**The Leader Inside**

## Praise for *The Leader Inside*

Lauren Kaufman guides us to better understand how we can make a meaningful difference in the lives of educators and children. Lauren reminds us that we all possess leadership qualities and that each interaction on our path is a lantern guiding us to our next destination. Through engaging stories, practical strategies, and insights, she helps us discover and recognize the gifts within ourselves and embrace the leader we are destined to be.

—**Jim Knight,** author of *The Definitive Guide to Instructional Coaching*

In her introduction, Lauren Kaufman poses a powerful question: "Have you thought about how you made it here?" This level of deep reflection sets the tone, reminding us that our experiences shape who we are, how we lead, and why our purpose must remain at the center of our decisions and actions. Kaufman's candid account of triumphs and setbacks empowers and motivates readers.

—**Mary Hemphill, PhD,** leadership expert and development coach

The more we research, the more we understand that leadership, like happiness, is not an individual sport. Our potential is interlinked with our beliefs and our ecosystem. In *The Leader Inside*, Kaufman describes how to tap into both to take the cap off of our potential to help others.

—**Shawn Achor,** bestselling author of *Big Potential*

As a woman in leadership, I found so many important reminders throughout *The Leader Inside* about the value of failing (and trying again—never give up, ladies!), the importance of a network of strong, brilliant women, and concrete strategies for building teacher efficacy, nurturing relationships, and finding balance amid real challenges in education. Kaufman's insights on stepping into leadership roles resonate deeply, highlighting the opportunity to elevate and celebrate educators and improve student outcomes by returning to our roots as teachers and nurturers.

—**Katie Novak, Ed.D.**, best-selling author, founder and executive director of Novak Education

Lauren Kaufman is a force of nature in the education space, and *The Leader Inside* is the book I've been waiting for her to write, with leadership lessons anyone can learn from, ideas that are actionable and easy to implement, and down-to-earth stories we can all relate to. A must-read book!

—**Adam Welcome,** international keynote speaker, author, educator, and podcaster

*The Leader Inside* is a powerful exploration of leadership through personal narratives and transformative insights. Kaufman, in conjunction with other inspiring voices, illustrates how diverse paths shape our identities as leaders, the critical role of mentorship in embracing one's potential, and the profound impact of courageous self-discovery. Through heartfelt stories and actionable ideas, readers are encouraged to embrace their inner leader as they navigate their unique paths to greatness. This book is an essential read for anyone aspiring to lead with both impact and authenticity.

—**Thomas C. Murray,** director of innovation, Future Ready Schools, best-selling author

Women in leadership have been the foundation of our schools and communities for many decades. They deserve to be elevated and empowered to continue to impact others. In *The Leader Inside*, Lauren Kaufman does just that! This book is the guide we have all been looking for to inspire us to continue in the fight for all of our students and teachers.

—**Salome Thomas-EL, Ed.D**, award-winning principal, speaker, and author

Leadership is about courage, humility, authenticity, integrity, and vision. Lauren personifies all of these qualities, and it is reflected in this wonderful, uplifting, and insightful book.

—**Dr Richard Gerver,** world-renowned speaker and author

Having been a fan of Lauren Kaufman's work for years, I eagerly anticipated reading her book. I was blown away by Lauren's stories of the transformative power of mentorship in the lives of educators and students. I highly recommend this book for any educator because all educators are leaders and all educators have the power to transform the lives of students and colleagues with a tap on the shoulder.

—**Allyson Apsey,** educational leader, author, national keynote speaker

This is an outstanding resource, whether you have been doing it for twenty years or five.

—**Joe Sanfelippo,** author and speaker

Through authentic and heartwarming stories, Kaufman shares her leadership journey, offering invaluable lessons along the way. The book masterfully blends her experiences with those of other powerful female leaders, creating a rich tapestry of practical advice and guidance. Want to feel empowered? The thought-provoking messages in this book will inspire readers to reflect on their own experiences and explore new perspectives.

—**Livia Chan,** head teacher, author, blogger, speaker

Lauren's capacity to humbly share her own story while highlighting the stories of others has produced an incredible book that will have a significant impact for years to come. As a superintendent, I appreciate that this book will resonate with school leaders, coaches, and teachers. The focus on women in leadership roles, self-discovery, growth, and valuing people makes this an excellent read for everyone in education.

—**Deidre Roemer,** superintendent

Prepare to have multiple highlighters and sticky notes on hand as you read a book filled with wisdom, insight, and actionable steps to enhance your leadership. *The Leader Inside* is the book that all aspiring and current school leaders need now.

—**Sean Gaillard,** author, podcaster, keynote speaker, and school leader

*The Leader Inside* uncovers the essence of authentic leadership. Rich with inspiring stories and practical strategies, it empowers readers to navigate their personal and professional journeys with confidence and resilience. This book is a must-read for anyone aspiring to lead with impact and integrity.

—**Katie Martin, PhD**, co-founder of Learner-Centered Collaborative and author of *Evolving Education* and *Learner-Centered Innovation*

Lauren Kaufman's *The Leader Inside* masterfully weaves together inspiring stories of mentorship, highlighting the transformative power of genuine connections and thoughtful guidance. This book is a beacon for educators and leaders, offering practical strategies and heartfelt insights to help you uncover and nurture the leader within

—**Joshua Stamper,** director of innovation for the Teach Better Team

# The Leader Inside

Stories of *Mentorship* to Inspire the *Leader Within*

**LAUREN M. KAUFMAN**

*The Leader Inside: Stories of Mentorship to Inspire the Leader Within*
© 2024 Lauren M. Kaufman

All rights reserved. No part of this publication may be reproduced in any form or by any electronic or mechanical means, including information storage and retrieval systems, without permission in writing by the publisher, except by a reviewer who may quote brief passages in a review. For information regarding permission, contact the publisher at books@impressbooks.org.

> This book is available at special discounts when purchased in quantity for educational purposes or for use as premiums, promotions, or fundraisers. For inquiries and details, contact the publisher at books@impressbooks.org.

Published by IMPress, a division of Dave Burgess Consulting, Inc.
IMPressbooks.org
DaveBurgessConsulting.com
San Diego, CA

Paperback ISBN: 978-1-948334-75-4
Ebook ISBN: 978-1-948334-76-1

Cover and interior design by Liz Schreiter
Edited and produced by Reading List Editorial
ReadingListEditorial.com

*To my mentors, who recognized the leader inside me from the start. Your belief and guidance illuminated my path. This book is a tribute to your wisdom, support, and love.*

*Mom and Dad, you have been a constant source of love and inspiration throughout my life.*

*I am immensely proud to be your daughter. Thank you for nurturing and supporting me as I discover the leader within. You've not only been my parents but also the epitome of what natural leaders should be.*

*Josh, your encouragement and support has anchored my writing journey. Drew and Ethan, I am committed to making you as proud as you make me every single day. My deepest wish for both of you is that you encounter people along your journey who recognize the exceptional leaders that live within you.*

# Contents

1   Introduction by Lauren M. Kaufman

## Part I: The Path to the Leader Inside

15   Chapter One: Unleashing Greatness from Within
by Lauren M. Kaufman

23   Chapter Two: Changing Lanes Without Signaling
by Lainie Rowell

31   Chapter Three: Finding Joy in the In-Between
by Stephanie Rothstein

38   Chapter Four: From Teacher to Leader
by Lauren M. Kaufman

## Part II: Mentors Are All Around Us

53   Chapter Five: Mentorship Matters
by Lauren M. Kaufman

61   Chapter Six: Stepping into Leadership
by Lauren M. Kaufman

71   Chapter Seven: Mentors Are All Around Us
by Lauren M. Kaufman

80   Chapter Eight: Mirrors Shape Leaders
by Lauren M. Kaufman

## Part III: Stories of Impact and Courage

92   Chapter Nine: The Leader Inside
by Lauren M. Kaufman

| | |
|---|---|
| 101 | Chapter Ten: Through the Glass Ceiling<br>by Natasha Nurse |
| 112 | Chapter Eleven: Eternal Memories Manifest Hope for the Future<br>by Lauren M. Kaufman and Linda Roth |
| 126 | Chapter Twelve: Be Your Own Champion<br>by Meghan Lawson |
| 133 | Moving Forward: Your Impact Moves with You<br>by Lauren M. Kaufman |

145 Endnotes
148 About Lauren M. Kaufman
150 Acknowledgments
153 More books from IMPress

# Introduction

### LAUREN M. KAUFMAN

Have you thought about how you made it here? Yes, here. To this moment. Holding this very book. It landed in your hands because it was meant to. Chances are that you opened it because you are serving in a formal leadership role, or you're thinking about stepping into one. Perhaps you find yourself naturally taking the lead in any role in which you serve, and you are gradually discovering the leader that lives inside you.

Education is the most gratifying career I can think of. Since you are reading this book, I think you feel that, too. You touch the hearts and minds of the kids, colleagues, and communities you serve. You are writing your own legacy and choosing how you will be remembered by touching the lives of others in intentional ways. Every interaction you are living, big and small, matters. A simple moment, a microcosm of your day, has the possibility of leaving a lasting impression. The idea that the people who cross your path could take a piece of you with them is special. Your impact and influence can be infinite. *How many other careers have the potential to leave a lasting impression and influence how people approach their future?*

## Part I: The Path to the Leader Inside

In Part I of this book, you will explore the heartfelt stories of women leaders and their unique paths to leadership. They will show you that there is not one path for us all to follow; each journey is unique. As you delve more deeply into these narratives, you'll recognize that our personal paths intricately shape our identities as leaders and provide us with a guiding compass. Within each chapter, you'll find profound lessons and actionable ideas tailored to empower you in your own journey to leadership. Let these insights resonate as you fearlessly navigate your way, forging a path to greatness that reflects the extraordinary leader that lives within you.

## Part II: Mentors Are All Around Us

In Part II of this book, you will read a collection of stories about the importance of mentors on the path to leadership, for both educators and leaders. This section highlights the truth that teaching and leading is not just a job, but a calling. Mentors are crucial for building on the strengths of educators and leaders while providing them with support for continuous growth and development. Mentors can be found in unexpected places. Seeking out mentors and support systems and taking advantage of your organization's mentor program can ground your purpose and emotions. It will also ignite your passion, especially when navigating new and unfamiliar environments. You will learn that no matter what role you serve in education, you are a mentor and leader. The impact of mentorship can help you discover untapped leadership qualities and unlock leadership opportunities, thanks to the people who have been placed in your path along the way. The guidance of strong mentors can uncover the leadership qualities you may not have seen in yourself! Unearthing these hidden leadership qualities can broaden your horizons and open doors to unimagined opportunities, thus providing you with the platform to achieve your highest potential.

## Part III: Stories of Impact and Courage

In Part III of this book, you will be immersed in stories of impact and courage. They illuminate how educators have found the leader that always lived inside them; there were many people on their path that supported their growth and development, but ultimately it was their own determination and perseverance that allowed them to break through barriers and rise to positions of influence. These women were given opportunities to lead early on in their lives, even when they didn't realize that those opportunities would shape the leader they are becoming. These experiences paved the way for them to build their confidence as they grew into the women leaders they were destined to become. Their stories will inspire and empower you to recognize your own potential for leadership and to overcome any obstacles that may stand in your way.

## Stories Are Signposts

All of your experiences have influenced your story. Each chapter has served as a guide, a signpost helping you row toward your next destination. The people who have lived inside your stories are likely the same people who have illuminated the leader inside you. My hope is that you have encountered many teachers, students, administrators, parents, caregivers, and community members who lifted you higher, made you smile bigger, and shaped your path to self-discovery.

As I have navigated over four decades of living and close to two decades in education, I have lived the stories that propelled me to be the leader I am becoming. I was born into a family of educators. My grandfather, my parents, my sister, and I all have stories to tell. Although each story is unique and special, mine is a little different, as the first person in my family to step into a formal leadership role. Along with my family, there have been people who paved a path for my development and growth as a human being, educator, and leader. Some walked into my life for moments, some for minutes, some for hours, some for days, and some for years. Some are more present than others, some have come and gone, while others have remained by my side. They have seen me through small and big wins, helped me navigate the obstacles I have faced, and valued me for the person I am, not the title under which I served. They are all important because they have shown me who I want and don't want to be. For that, I am truly grateful.

There were many people on my path who recognized the leader inside me. Years later, I can still hear my high school sophomore class adviser, Mrs. Millman, who was also my guidance counselor, propose a leadership opportunity to me. "Lauren, you are going to choreograph the dances for the Battle of the Classes Dance Competition," she told me.

"Um . . . me?" I replied. I could feel my face hurting as it got red and hot. Simultaneously, I was smiling big, startled by the surprise vote of confidence. This was a huge school event where all the classes competed against one another in several competitions. Every person competing took the event very seriously. One of the biggest events was the dance competition, and I was going to be in charge of its fate? I'll admit, I have some good rhythm, but let me be clear, I am no professional dancer!

"Yes, you. I can see how you can rally people together in a humble way. People listen to you and take your guidance. I watch your classmates approach you for advice. You can do this, and you will be great. You're a leader."

Fifteen years later, and about nine years into my teaching career, when I was serving as an elementary school reading specialist, I remember being "tapped on the shoulder" by a colleague to apply for the instructional coaching position in my former district. "Lauren, what do you think about applying for the instructional coaching role?" she asked. "I think you would be really good at it. You already wear a coaching hat as a reading specialist. You're always supporting teachers with your expertise and providing them with high-quality resources.

You even model lessons in classrooms. Not much will change. You should go for it. You're a leader."

I can still hear my former principal when I was an instructional coach, Mrs. Karen Sauter, saying, "Lauren, you know you have to go for your leadership credential. A formal leadership position will be your next step. I can see what you're capable of accomplishing. You are making a difference. You're a leader."

A few years after that, I can remember the familiar, reassuring voice of my fourth-grade teacher, Mrs. Linda Roth. It was over thirty years later, and we kept in touch. Yes, this example is a testament to the legacy she imparted. Mrs. Roth's journey in education led her to retiring as an assistant superintendent for curriculum and instruction. Our true mentors never really leave us, do they? They are always with us and can come back into our lives at just the right times. More stories on mentorship later!

Mrs. Roth recognized my leadership qualities as a little girl, and now she was preparing me for my first administrative interviews. As I navigated several interview processes, I found out that I was passed over for a few positions I really hoped to get. This came after making it through several intense rounds in a rigorous interview process. I can still hear her voice wrapping around my crushed spirit, saying, "Lauren, this is all a part of the process. THIS rejection, THIS disappointment pressing on your heart. THIS feeling right now is a fleeting moment in time. THIS is your door to a new beginning. THIS is your time to choose a new door that will open another opportunity and you WILL have the choice to make. That's because you're a leader."

During all this, I recall a close colleague and friend saying, "Lauren, use this interaction, this story, this failed interview to fuel you. You are more than this moment in time, and it is going to just take the right people to see it. You're a leader." But more about interviews later!

I share these stories for a reason. Each of the people I've encountered on my educational journey made me realize something important for myself and others. It's the idea that you do not have to reflect what someone thinks you should be. Instead, you can be a reflection of the person YOU want and are meant to be.

We all have our "path to leadership" stories. Stories are windows into the soul. They are hidden treasures buried beneath a sea of hopes, wishes, and dreams. They are small moments in time that pass you by. They are memories that enrapture your heart and wrap around your spirit. They are the hidden paths to who you were, who you are, and who you are destined to become. You are a collection of invisible stories, strung together and concealed by your external being. Stories bind us to people. They are entry points to connection and open pathways to your learning journey. They shape your core identity; they reflect your perception, your values, and what you stand for. Stories are windows into our experiences. They are the fuel that pushes you down the path to self-fulfillment. Your stories are living in mind memory boxes, waiting to be courageously unwrapped and gifted to people who will use them to discover ideas and recognize their own passions.

In an episode of his *Innovator's Mindset* podcast, George Couros brilliantly says, "Stories are the fuel for innovation. They inspire us, they give us pertinent ideas, they get the work we are doing out to people in a really compelling way that goes beyond what a score could tell people about our students."[1] Beneath the facade of every human being lies a personal, unique collection of stories that reveal reflections of who they are and who they want to be.

*Where are you creating spaces for educators to share how they found their path to education and leadership through stories?*

I wrote this book because I want others to see that we all have the potential to be the person we are destined to become. Many of the people who live inside my own stories and on my personal path to leadership are women leaders who have empowered me, cheered me on, celebrated my successes, and lifted me up when I needed it most (even when I didn't know it). They recognized that my gifts were meant to be shared with others. Because of the people placed in my path, I know there is a leader living inside us all.

INTRODUCTION

## **Lessons in Women's Leadership**

Not long ago, I was invited to join a group of inspiring women leaders to speak about my story, and the path that led me to leadership, at an educational event. Amid the buzz of excitement, I found myself in the center of a bustling, standing-room-only room, surrounded by influential women and educators from different backgrounds. Upbeat music set the tone for a moment of reflection as I pondered how I had reached this point in my career, the pivotal role of those who believed in my potential, and the significance of being a person of influence.

These questions circled my mind in a matter of seconds: *How did I get here? Who helped me recognize my potential and why didn't others? When did I become a person of influence? Am I supposed to be here?* The energy in the room was palpable, and the audience's backgrounds in education were vast. They ranged from the novice teacher exploring her own path and potential in education to the veteran teacher leaders and administrators looking for a dose of inspiration and invigoration. They all fostered a sense of support and empowerment. Although it was clear that the room was overflowing, it did not deter more and more women (and some men) from walking in and standing along the perimeter of the space or taking their seat on the floor—the only place available.

And then we started. Little preparation went into this Women in Leadership session. It started with a few leaders embracing the idea and then asking others to join. A slide deck was shared, and each leader added a quote, a few pictures, and a book suggestion. One leader opened the session by talking about how leadership can be challenging and the importance of finding other women leaders to support you through it all.

One by one, ten women I admire shared their stories, their paths to leadership, with vulnerability and grace. One story was rooted in perseverance as this leader battled an illness at the beginning of her principalship. Another described the years of interviewing and battling rejection it took to find the right fit. Another shared the challenges of

7

navigating motherhood and leadership. I hung onto their every word, and so did the audience. I know that because it is an unspoken rule at this event that you may leave the session if it's not serving your needs and no judgment is passed. Not one person left. In fact, people who heard buzz about the session in real time were standing outside the door to capture the powerful messages being shared.

Later, we opened the session up to participants, and they felt compelled and empowered to share their personal stories about their own pathways to leadership. The session could have easily lasted all day as people lingered in the room to approach each leader and thank them for their courage. There were a lot of connections made in that hour, along with lots of tears shed. This was the next generation of leaders in the making.

In an *Education Week* article titled "7 Ways Districts Can Increase the Number of Women Leaders" by Denisa R. Superville, several female district leaders were interviewed. Superville emphasized that leveraging current female leaders to inspire the next generation is critical. LaTanya McDade, one of the female leaders interviewed and the superintendent for Prince William County Public Schools in Virginia, shared the following sentiment: "Representation matters, and so that is the weight that I carry as a woman in leadership: understanding that I have to be a model for those who will come after me, as well as honor those who have come before me, who have allowed me to be able to have this opportunity. It's not a responsibility that I take lightly."[2]

When I reflected on this session, I thought about how I didn't know all the women who shared personally but felt like I did. I also noticed that all the women had something in common: they were all models for the next generation of female leaders who authentically gave recognition to others. Their lens on leadership did not project a feeling of "I," but a collective responsibility of "we."

When it was my turn to speak that day, I shared part of my story: "Getting to the place I am now did not come easily. It took some pretty amazing people to recognize my strengths and pick me up during the times when I had fallen down. There have been many remarkable moments in my career, but there have also been some disappointments. You see, you need those moments, too. They support your personal evolution, your path to transformation. They help you see that happiness doesn't just exist in where we are, it lives in what we have to do to get there."

## Where Do You Want to Be?

So, I ask, "Where are you now, and where do you want to be?" In his book *Atomic Habits*, James Clear says, "Your life bends in the direction of your habits. Every action you take is a vote for the person you want to become."[3] When I reflect on my past and present experiences, I often ask myself, *Who is the leader you wish to become, Lauren?* My answer is, *I wish to become the leader I always needed.* No matter where your journey takes you, your actions create a collection of stories that can positively impact others.

Stories are lenses that formulate perspectives and cultivate community. They are sound bites, and short episodes of our lives. They are opportunities to personalize classroom and professional learning experiences, make connections to new learning, and build a bridge that connects us with people to form new ideas. In *Personal and Authentic: Designing Learning Experiences That Impact a Lifetime*, Thomas C. Murray wrote, "Weaving together our experiences creates our story, makes us who we are, and determines the context in which we each learn."[4] Understanding and sharing our own stories and the stories within our school organizations forges deeper connections that lead to deeper learning.

Understanding stories also values the uniqueness of each individual and brings purpose to authentic work. As we proceed with our lives, we will encounter new opportunities and people who are waiting to meet us. Although every person has guided my direction, we all have the divine power to choose our own path, our ultimate destination. We can take our experiences, our stories, our lessons learned to bring our hopes and dreams to fruition. *What will you do to intentionally shape the narratives you want to create and write the stories you want to be a part of?*

> As you embark on this journey through the pages of this book, I extend an open invitation to engage with the greater educational community and myself:
>
> - Share your thoughts, ideas, quotes that resonate, and questions using the hashtag **#TheLeaderInside**.
> - Tag me on social media platforms (@LaurenMKaufman) or connect with me through my website, LaurenMKaufman.com.
>
> Let's continue to connect, recognize each other's gifts, and build a thriving community of learners and leaders who inspire each other along the way!

The stories I've shared, coupled with my personal experiences and stories of strong female leaders, inspired me to write and thoughtfully curate this book. I want to emphasize that the handful of contributors whose voices are illuminated here are women I know both personally and professionally. They have taken me under their wing, believed in my abilities, and mentored, coached, and guided me. And now, they can be pillars of hope and inspiration for you, too. I adore how they've captured their personal path to leadership with vulnerability, beauty, and grace. You might notice that no story is linear or the same. There is not one particular guide leaders use to find success. If there was, we'd all be using it. Instead, we use a collection of experiences, advice, and stories to lead us to where we need to be.

Within each chapter, you will find "Actionable Ideas to Implement Tomorrow." I encourage you to reflect on these ideas or formulate your own in book clubs and staff meetings, and within your leadership teams and classrooms. You may even consider gifting this book to educators who need a dose of inspiration and courage as they pursue their hopes and dreams. Cross-pollinate these ideas and implement them in ways that best meet your personal and professional goals. Let this book be a source of inspiration for your soul and lead you to fulfilling your leadership aspirations. Let our collective voices allow you to reflect on the narrative you wish to create and guide you to your next destination. Allow this book to be what you need it to be, and let it help you rediscover the leader inside. Here. We. Go.

## PART I:

# The Path to the Leader Inside

CHAPTER ONE

# Unleashing Greatness from Within

## BY LAUREN M. KAUFMAN

> *I've come to believe that each of us has a personal calling that's as unique as a fingerprint—and that the best way to succeed is to discover what you love and then find a way to offer it to others in the form of service, working hard, and also allowing the energy of the universe to lead you.*
>
> —OPRAH WINFREY

The heartbeat of education lives inside the walls of schools. Within those walls you can find stories of kids and teachers in the mess of learning. You will watch students, teachers, administrators, and staff buzzing about the halls and classrooms igniting discussion, cultivating curiosity, instilling joy, leading with empathetic hearts, and smiling through it all. The epicenter of those learning spaces will captivate and inspire you to listen more intently. You will see new things and look through lenses you may have not considered before. You don't have to search for the big things to see good things happen. The small things matter, too.

Time spent immersed in classrooms, and the relationships you develop in school, are the most valuable growth experiences you can have as an educational leader.

I often reminisce about my days in the classroom. When I became an educator, I wanted to show my students what they were capable of accomplishing. I wanted to help them find their voices and discover their inner leaders; I wanted to provide a sense of hope that would continuously stir within. Inside my classroom walls, we found stories and moments of impact that shaped the educator and leader I am becoming today. Although my path to leadership began when I was a young girl, my bigger leadership lessons happened in the classroom. Those ideas and stories reflect the experiences I'd later learn from and take with me as I embarked on new paths. They were opportunities to personalize learning experiences, and the bridge that connected me to people. Within those walls, I learned from myself and others to embrace my own gifts so I could help my students and colleagues find theirs.

Within every role you serve are opportunities that invite you to think about the educator you were and who you want to be. Over time, you establish and develop relationships, garner a multitude of teaching and learning practices, take part in numerous conversations, and make an impact on countless families, colleagues, and students who were destined to know you. It can be exciting to think about a team of people you have not yet met, who will eventually become a constant in your life. Or perhaps some people will enter your life for a short time and create pathways to opportunities you don't yet know exist. Every experience you will ever have leads to the type of educator you wish to become.

I have always looked to teacher leaders and administrators to model high-leverage practices I can bring back to my students and colleagues. *Have you ever observed the leaders who authentically appreciate, trust, and value the people they serve?* Those leaders have an innate gift for developing and unleashing the greatness within every person they encounter. They inspire others to humbly give their hearts and minds to others and make contributions to something that matters. I often think about the leaders who breathed life into my ideas, trusted me to bring those ideas to fruition, and unlocked the potential I didn't know I had. For that, I'm eternally grateful.

In Brené Brown's *Dare to Lead* podcast, Adam Grant shared, "The most meaningful way to succeed is to help other people succeed."[5] Grant went on to explain that you cannot be considered a high performer in an organization if you don't make other people better. *Could shining the light on others, honoring who they really are, challenging them to do the hard things, and instilling a courageous spirit pave a path that shows others the leaders they are meant to be?* Focusing on what it means for people to enhance one another's successes while elevating each other's strong attributes can lead to collective success. In turn, this builds a stronger culture and impacts who is at the heart of all our efforts—kids! There is a certain kind of excitement in inspiring others. As Stephen Covey shares in his book *Trust and Inspire*, "When people feel that their work matters, they feel that *they* matter."[6]

When I was a new teacher, I worked for the New York City Department of Education as a classroom teacher. I adored my first principal, Mrs. Beth Longo. She gave me my first foot in the door when I had little experience in education. I elaborate more on this story in the book *Because of a Teacher*.[7] She was a mentor who saw the leader in me. Beth had high expectations, was honest in her feedback, pushed her teachers to try new practices, and gave them the courage to self-reflect. She knew her teachers well because she made herself visible by opening classroom doors. She was direct in her approach while remaining endearing all at once.

One day, Beth pulled me into her office and said, "Lauren, our district superintendent is visiting our school tomorrow with her team, and I am going to bring them into your classroom." What happened next? I stared at her without answering. I could feel the confused look on my usually rosy-turned-pale face. She interrupted my silence by saying, "Lauren, I know you're thinking that since you are a new teacher, I shouldn't be bringing these people into your classroom. Is that why you aren't answering me? That's what you are thinking, isn't it?" I finally blinked. "Well . . . ummm . . . hmmmm. Maybe?" She interrupted me again. "Lauren, I'll see you in your classroom tomorrow. Just do me a favor—be yourself and smile." In that moment, I could feel the rosiness restoring to my pale cheeks and my heart rate returning to a normal beat. That night, I spent an enormous amount of time lesson planning and prepping for one of the most nerve-racking experiences that any teacher, but especially a NEW teacher, can endure. I think you know that no matter how perfect your lesson plan can be, there has never been a lesson in the history of lessons that unfolded exactly as intended.

## Helping Others Succeed

The next day, my classroom instantly became a lab site, a revolving door. As I stood in the middle of my classroom, teaching and learning with my students, administrators who were strangers took their places around the perimeter of my classroom. It felt like we were in a theater-in-the-round. Out of the corner of my eye, I saw several guests approach my students. I remember them asking, "What are you learning today?" To this very day, I don't remember my guests' faces or every interaction that happened in that room. What I do remember is what it felt like to be challenged and a good pressure to rise to the occasion by just being myself. I also vividly recall the conversation I had with Beth after the experience. She asked me, "Lauren, what did you learn about yourself as an educator today?" I paused, and the first thing I said was, "I can do hard things while being myself." She came back with another question: "Lauren, what did you learn from today that you can take with you for the rest of your career?" I smiled with a sense of relief and replied, "I need time to think about that, Beth. Can I have some time to reflect?"

It is nearly two decades later, and I am now serving as a district administrator. In the beginning of this chapter, I shared that I got into education because I wanted to show my students what they were capable of. Now it's my turn to show educators what they are capable of, to help them find their voices, to discover the leader inside.

So, if you are like me, and continuing on your leadership path, consider opening the doors to schools and classrooms. You will find so much goodness living there. Although you may not have a classroom to call your own, you can still find ways to step into the mess of learning. When you miss the moments of impact you experienced with your own students, take a leap of faith and open a classroom door. Recently, I walked through one and was greeted by a teacher with the warmest, most genuine smile. "Look at that smile," I said. The teacher replied, "Well, it matches yours, Lauren." Once again, I was reminded that the small things, like walking through a classroom door with a smile, are really the big things. In *Because of a Teacher, Volume II*, George Couros said, "What is so amazing about education as a profession is that what you do impacts people who later go out and impact people. In this sense, teachers will never get the recognition they deserve because their impact can be infinite."[8]

As a district leader, the opportunities to have an infinite impact and influence on colleagues and students can become more limited (if I let them). After all, the regular proximity to staff and students that comes with being a building leader may not be as readily available. So, I regularly ask myself, *How can I find ways to continuously expand my impact and broaden my influence as an instructional leader?* I have come to understand that impact and influence lives in every level of an organization. It's the people in systems that have the potential to do amazing things.

## Finding the Greatness Within

I am still thinking about Beth's last question. If I were to answer what I learned from that experience today, I would respond with this: "Great leaders can help others find their gifts and light a spark that ignites a sense of passion and purpose. They give you just the right amount of push, believe in you to grow into the leader you are destined to be, and encourage you to be the best version of yourself." In his book *How to Know a Person: The Art of Seeing Others Deeply and Being Deeply Seen*, David Brooks shares the following: "I often ask people to tell me about times they've felt seen, and with glowing eyes, they tell me stories about pivotal moments in their life. They talk about a time when someone perceived some talent in them that they themselves weren't even able to see."[9]

Considering these profound reflections, Stephen Covey shares the following sentiment and question in *Trust and Inspire*: "Instead of asking why aren't my people motivated? A better question to ask yourself is—How can I better inspire those I lead?"[10] This perspective has a strong connection with Brooks's insights about the influence of stories, leadership, and perception, illuminating the crucial role leaders play in unlocking potential and inspiring growth within individuals. As you proceed on your leadership journey, take a step into opportunities that can transform educators' mindsets by letting them experience what it feels like to garner courage and step into hard things. There are future leaders waiting for you to recognize their innate gifts and unleash their greatness within.

## Actionable Ideas to Implement Tomorrow

As I evolve into the instructional leader I wish to become, I think about my interactions with great leaders like Beth. I have committed to the following ideas to help expand my impact and broaden my influence within the walls of schools:

- **Be Human-Centered:** Connections are cornerstones to our hearts. Recognize that educators are people first and learn what they care about outside the walls of education.
- **Lead with Empathy:** Begin conversations by acknowledging other people's humanity. Ask about their well-being and family, and show

genuine interest in their answers. Listen actively and without judgment to grasp their emotions and perspectives. Prioritize understanding over swift problem-solving during discussions. Empathize with their experiences, validate their emotions, and provide personalized support. Guide and support them by being responsive rather than reactive to their needs. Sometimes it is best to take some time and think things through before responding. Then, following up with specificity significantly enhances relationship investment, reflection, and rapport.

- **Provide Thoughtful Feedback:** Use a coaching lens and ask questions that will lead people to finding their own answers to challenges. Then give feedback that will elevate their ideas such as: "It sounds like you . . ." and "I am wondering if . . ." Elena Aguilar from the Bright Morning Team has powerful coaching stems to help guide those conversations.[11]
- **Recognize the Gifts in Others:** Listen to people attentively. You will discover their strengths and areas of expertise. Develop those gifts and capitalize on their knowledge to cross-pollinate ideas across an organization.
- **Keep Kids at the Heart of Decision-Making:** When you keep the conversations focused on what is best for kids' social, emotional, and intellectual growth, your impact and influence will touch the lives of many students even though you may not directly work with them.

**Lainie Rowell** is a best-selling author, award-winning educator, and TEDx speaker. An experienced teacher and district leader, she is dedicated to human flourishing, focusing on community building, social emotional learning, and honoring what makes each of us unique and dynamic through learner-driven design. She earned her degree in psychology and went on to earn postgraduate degrees in education. As an international keynoter and a consultant, Lainie's client list ranges from Fortune 100 companies like Apple and Google to school districts and independent schools. She is the author of *Evolving with Gratitude*, the lead author of *Evolving Learner*, and a contributing author to *Because of a Teacher*. Her latest, *Bold Gratitude: The Journal Designed for You & by You*, is an innovative and interactive journal empowering individuals of all ages to express gratitude uniquely. Lainie's work has been highlighted in many publications, including Edutopia, *Thrive Global*, *ASCD K-12 Leadership SmartBrief*, *Getting Smart*, and *PBS NewsHour*. Since 2014, Lainie has been a consultant for the Orange County Department of Education's Institute for Leadership Development. You can see what she's up to on the socials using @LainieRowell and on her website, LainieRowell.com.

CHAPTER TWO

# Changing Lanes Without Signaling

### BY LAINIE ROWELL

*Embrace your life journey with gratitude, so that how you travel your path is more important than reaching your ultimate destination.*

—ROSALENE GLICKMAN

If, at any point in my first twenty years on this planet, you had told me that I would end up as an educator, a leader, and a content creator, I would have laughed. And I mean out loud, doubled over trying to catch my breath, possibly with an unpleasant snort or two.

I was not what you would call a "strong student." Don't get me wrong, I loved to learn, but I never understood how to do school like others did. I was able to squeak by with grades that were acceptable to my parents and even went to college as *they* dreamed I would (clearly college acceptance wasn't as competitive back then), but how I longed for the days when I would get out of school.

I should say, for as long as I can remember, I've been fascinated by the human mind and behavior. So, when it came time to pick a major, psychology was an obvious choice. And it didn't hurt that it had fewer requirements than most, so graduating in four years was a real possibility (if you went year-round, like I did). Are you picking up on how motivated I was to get out of school? I get it–the joke's on me.

Here's where the road takes a significant turn. As part of earning my psych degree, I was required to do field hours. I had a variety of options to complete this requirement: a hospital, a community center, a school, etc. You may see where this is going. Yes, I chose the school. If I'm being honest, it was the only option that was within walking distance of campus. Little did I know, my laziness and love of efficiency would pay off because as soon as I set foot in that classroom and was introduced to the amazing child I would be working with, I knew I wanted to be a teacher.

No doubt, my family must have thought I was changing lanes without signaling. After all, their daughter, who constantly complained about school and vocalized other interests, enlisting in postgraduate work to earn her teaching credential?!? But I made it happen, and it was easily one of the best decisions of my life.

I share this embarrassing, important part of my story because, as I zoom along on my journey as an educator and leader, I can see that the road I'm traveling has been marked by signals and signposts. Some were events, like choosing to do my hours at a school, but most had to do with someone believing in me even when I couldn't see my own potential. Their faith in me propelled me forward in ways I couldn't even imagine.

Specifically, these caring guides saw strengths in me that I didn't, and here's what I know now: when someone sees something great in you and takes the time to share it, believe them! Not only that, lean into it.

Looking back on my first twenty-five-plus years in education, I see three major roles I've had the honor and privilege of serving in thanks to these guides: innovative classroom educator, professional learning leader, and content creator. And here are some of the important milestones so far (potholes and other road hazards included).

## Innovative Classroom Educator: Kicked Out of My Comfort Zone

In my third year as an educator, I was teaching first grade at a school I LOVED! Seriously, it was a teacher's dream come true: strong leadership, a collaborative team, kiddos eager to learn, and families who had our backs. But the district was opening a new school, which meant my school, where I had worked hard to get to teach, would be reducing its numbers. The following year, about half the students moved to the new school. And, you know the drill, fewer students means fewer teachers. As a newbie, I knew I'd be the first to go. I had two choices: be involuntarily transferred to another school in the district or apply for the new school. With little hope of success, I opted for the latter.

I can still picture that moment when I walked into the portable classroom serving as the temporary school office. (The new school wasn't even built yet. I'm talking about exposed two-by-fours, A-frames, and dirt everywhere!) I interviewed with the new principal, Monique. She asked me a series of standard interview questions. Then she asked the tech questions. Eeek! I was a total tech neophyte. I admitted as much, and it was her next question that sealed the deal and made me want to follow this leader to the ends of the earth. She said, "Are you willing to learn? We will all be learning together." I was sold and, to my surprise, I was hired.

## Professional Learning Leader: A Recovering Squeaky Wheel

This new school was designed for innovation with technology. We didn't have a lot of tech, but what we had was the latest and greatest, and I was excited to learn. Monique encouraged all of us to do as much learning as possible AND to share! If you went to a conference, you brought what you learned back and presented it at a staff meeting. She also arranged for classes to be covered so we could visit each other's classrooms to model, co-teach, and see each other in practice.

She encouraged us to present at conferences and earn certifications. I jumped at every opportunity and voluntarily took on a ton of extra leadership tasks.

Even though I had taken on additional responsibilities by choice, I still stormed into Monique's office one day ranting about how I couldn't possibly be expected to teach full-time, lead professional learning regularly, and take on all these extra leadership tasks. Yikes, I was entitled and petulant. Thankfully, Monique was all grace and patience. She said, "So what is your proposal?" I stared at her completely befuddled. She explained, "Lainie, when you have a problem, I need you to come with some ideas so we can work together on the best possible solution." Monique was teaching me to be solution-oriented, not just a squeaky wheel. The next day I returned with ideas and we had a conversation. In the end, we came up with a plan that allowed me to stay in the classroom with my kiddos and have a little release time to support the staff school-wide without burning out. With Monique's guidance, I created a new role for myself, one that I didn't even know was an option. A couple years later, Monique's faith and coaching led to me landing a district leadership position. With her blessing, I accepted, and a whole new world opened up to me.

### Content Creator: I Raised My Hand

In 2006, I attended a conference with Alan November as the featured speaker. He asked if anyone in the audience was using technology to connect their students to students in other countries to cultivate a global perspective. I timidly raised my hand, and as I looked around, I noticed I was the only one (and turned bright red in the process). Alan also noticed I was the only one to raise my hand, and he approached me after his talk. We chatted, and he ended up inviting me to his Building Learning Communities (BLC) conference in Boston.

This next part is so bananas, I can't even believe it. It started with me being a guest at his inspiring international conference. It led to

Alan sending me to schools and districts around the world to share the importance of empowering students to own their learning. The best part was that I was often presenting with and learning from other educators. I grew so much!

And then, I got a call from Alan in August 2014. I can tell you exactly where I was standing in my backyard when I answered the call. It was surreal, to say the least. Alan was calling to invite me to keynote BLC 2015. And get this, he wanted me to talk about my work as a professional learning leader. (Cue the record scratching sound.) *Wait, what? I facilitate professional learning, I don't talk about professional learning.* Luckily, I kept those thoughts inside my head. And then I went meta. *What do I do that works?* I didn't stop there. *What do others do that works? What does the research say?*

This was not my first keynote and I was fully prepared, but I can honestly say I have never been more terrified to get on a stage. I probably wouldn't have even made it to the ballroom if it wasn't for a serious solo dance session in my hotel room to "Shake It Off" by Taylor Swift. (What can I say? It's a vibe!)

Alan gave me a generous introduction, I took the stage, and I went for it. To this day, I find it a bit cringy to watch myself speak, but it was such an out-of-body experience that I forced myself to watch just to confirm it really happened. I was shocked—my voice wasn't cracking and if I was shaking, it didn't show. Good thing, because little did I know, an editor from a well-known publisher was in the audience. She approached me afterward and suggested I write a book about professional learning. Five years later, my first book was published. And if, on the day that book was published, you had told me there would be more books to come, I would have laughed. Again, out loud, doubled over trying to catch my breath, possibly with an unpleasant snort or two.

There is more to the story of my journey to becoming a content creator and the road that lies ahead, but I will never forget that it all started with me raising my hand.

## Actionable Ideas to Implement Tomorrow

### You Don't Have to Wait for Signals and Signposts

These were just a few of the important milestones in my unique journey, and I realize I was blessed to have all these caring, inspiring guides along the way. I realize not everyone is fortunate to have so many people as signals and signposts. Here is my advice for you: find your own strengths and let them guide you.

Not sure where to start? I suggest taking the free VIA Survey of Character Strengths available at viacharacter.org. According to research, understanding and applying your strengths can help:

- boost confidence
- increase happiness
- strengthen relationships
- manage problems
- reduce stress
- accomplish goals
- build meaning and purpose
- improve work performance

Once you know your signature strengths, use the wisdom and knowledge shared in this book to put them into action!

### In Hindsight

If I could go back to twenty-year-old Lainie, I would say:

- Stepping out of your comfort zone is essential. Be grateful when it's forced upon you.
- When someone sees great things in you and takes the time to share it, believe them and lean into it.
- Be a problem-solver, and be bold enough to create your own path.
- Raise your hand proudly and put content out there that you believe in.
- You don't have to wait for others to see your strengths. You can find them yourself.
- Find joy and gratitude in the moment, in the process, and be present for it all rather than just checking off boxes and looking for the next thing.

- Give to others in a way that lifts them up, amplifies their voices, and makes their lives better.

## Moving Forward

I never would have guessed how I'd get here, so I won't pretend I know exactly what lies ahead. But I do know I'll continue learning with and from kids and my peers. I'll continue putting content I believe in out into the world. And now, more than ever, I'm focused on serving as a guide for others as they navigate their own unique road. I do this in honor of the many who served as signals and signposts on my journey. And while I can't name them all in the space provided, here are just a few: Jane Holm, Monique Huibregtse, Steve Glyer, Mike Lawrence, Alan November, Christine Olmstead, and George Couros.

I'll leave you with this wondering:

> *What if we all had the audacity to believe in ourselves as much as those who see greatness within us? What limitless possibilities would unfold if we were so bold?*

**Stephanie Rothstein** is an educational leader focused on making education more collaborative and less competitive. She advocates for modeling the risks we expect of our students and shared about this in her TEDx talk, "My Year of Yes to Me," published on Ted.com. She is focused on supporting growth in the following areas: design thinking, project-based learning,  cross-curricular pathway development, collaboration and communication, professional learning, and educational technology. Stephanie has been an educator for over twenty-two years, spending most of that time in a high school English classroom. Stephanie is a certified administrator and currently serves as an educational innovation leader for Santa Clara Unified School District, a K–12 school district supporting 15,500 students and over 1,000 teachers at thirty-one schools. She is a founder of GlobalGEG, the creator of CanWeTalkEDU, and the author of numerous articles published on Edutopia and her own blog. She speaks at educational conferences around the world and was named CUE's Teacher of the Year for 2021. Stephanie is a contributing author to *Because of a Teacher* by George Couros, published in 2021, and she also contributed to *Evolving with Gratitude* by Lainie Rowell, published in 2022. You can connect with Stephanie on X: @StephRothEDU.

CHAPTER THREE

# Finding Joy in the In-Between

## BY STEPHANIE ROTHSTEIN

*Fight for the things that you care about, but do it in a way that will lead others to join you.*

—RUTH BADER GINSBURG

In my seventeenth year as an educator, I split my time between teaching, chairing a project-based learning pathway, and being a TOSA (teacher on special assignment) for my school district. A district mentor who I respect very much, Carrie Bosco, asked me a question during a check-in meeting: "Do you want to be an administrator?"

"No! That was never my plan."

"Really? I think you would make a great administrator, and some of the best administrators I know never went into education thinking that was their goal."

I left that room pondering the journey I had been on. I consistently found myself balancing many roles at once, but administration had never been a goal. What I did know was this: I love supporting students, I love supporting teachers, and I love supporting impactful change. Over and over, I found that the kind of impact I wanted to have required an admin title. To my surprise, my mentor was right.

After talking it over with my husband and kids, I enrolled in an admin credential program the following year. I was surrounded by teachers in their fifth year of teaching who had always known that being an administrator was their goal, or at least that's how it felt. I'm happy for them, but that wasn't (and isn't) me. It's taken me time to be OK with this, and to feel like I understand how to share and be proud of my own educational leadership journey. And that is precisely what I want to share—*the journey that unlocked my understanding of what it means to be a leader.*

Starting my admin credential program sparked me to take on other challenges. I began writing and speaking at conferences and pursued experiences that focused on growing me as a leader. In 2019, I was accepted as a Google for Education Innovator. I traveled to Singapore for a life-changing experience with thirty-two other educators focused on creating impactful change in education. When asked for my job title at the Innovator Academy, I found myself unsure what to write on my name badge. How do I explain to people what I do in a meaningful way? The truth is, my role often sits somewhere in between that of a teacher and administrator, and my title never explains it well.

What I have come to accept now that I'm in my twenty-third year as an educator is that I actually love and value the in-between space. I didn't always feel that way because it's messy, and it isn't always easy, but it provides me with a freedom I haven't found in other positions. Currently, my title is District Innovation Leader, Innovation TOSA. I oversee district-level innovation projects and work with teachers to support them with professional learning and coaching.

At the start of this school year, I had an epiphany in a meeting with my supervisor.

"What are your goals for this school year?" they asked.

"My main goals are to grow and support teacher leadership, and grow the internal capacity of school sites."

"Can you explain why this is a priority and how it aligns with innovation?"

"I am the one person in this district with my title. I work with all thirty-one schools and there are twelve hundred educators here. I cannot do this work alone. And I need to be strategic in the work I do. Growing leadership will allow the projects to have impact. Otherwise, nothing will change and I'll burn out."

My journey is best illustrated through the projects I implemented to grow internal leadership.

## Step 1: Building Trust

### Project 1: EdTech Celebrations

Before I could grow leadership and move with people in any direction, I needed to connect with them and build trust. And to build trust, I needed to help them be seen and appreciated for all they were currently doing.

But how do you actually do that? How do you help people be seen and grow connections authentically? I had to create a way to see the great work they were doing in their classrooms firsthand, and allow other people to see it as well. So I implemented a project called EdTech Celebrations. I met with our reps from EdTech companies and asked them to give me swag. I asked the twelve companies who had accounts with the district, and they all sent me boxes of merch. Then, I made EdTech Rockstar thank-you cards and had them printed at our district print shop. I stuffed EdTech Celebration Swag Bags with the company swag (a mug, T-shirt, socks, pens, and more), popcorn and candy, and district-branded items (pennants, bags, and more). Every month, I delivered these swag bags to educators throughout the district. As part of our visits, we made district videos featuring these educators where they explained the impact of a particular tech application on student learning. I am proud to say that I delivered twenty bags every month, which got me into two hundred classrooms over the school year. I love that this project connected me with teachers, counselors, librarians, paraeducators, and administrators.

As the popularity of EdTech Celebrations grew, I found myself fielding questions about my time.

"Are you sure we shouldn't have someone else take this project over? We can get other people to deliver the swag bags if you want," my supervisor proposed as we mapped out my project time.

"No, this is worthy time, it's the worthiest time. This builds connections, it helps educators feel seen, and I am lucky that I get to do it. If it isn't me and if it isn't in person, the impact isn't the same."

The results:

- The EdTech Rock Stars who received swag bags reported that teachers on their own campus were coming to them, seeking out thought partnerships and support as they tried something new.
- At school sites where I delivered swag bags each month, I saw a drastic increase in usage of EdTech applications.
- These educators were the first to sign up for other professional learning opportunities in the school district, and they brought colleagues with them on their journey.

### Step 2: Growing Impact

### Project 2: Innovation Classroom Cohort

My leadership role is not only between titles; it's also between departments. I exist between Ed Services and Tech Services. I was hired to be the conduit between these departments. This can be complicated, but I have chosen to focus on the freedom and increased collaboration this provides.

The Innovation Classroom Cohort was born out of this collaboration, as a partnership between me, the director of professional learning, and the director of technology. The teachers who opted into the cohort had their classrooms outfitted with new technology: new audiovisual equipment, a television to replace their projector and screen, an iPad, student and teacher microphones, and more. My role was to map out the entire year of professional learning and provide the teachers with a year of coaching support.

The first year of the cohort, we had fifteen middle school teachers. We held a combination of full-day in-person sessions and virtual after-school sessions. In person we focused on goal setting, lesson/unit planning, technology training, and teacher collaboration. I led the in-person days and brought in a variety of experts for the virtual sessions.

A favorite component of the teacher collaboration was Light Bulb Talks, which were based on presentation types we had seen at other conferences: Spark Talks, Booms, Pecha Kucha–style presentations, etc. We asked participants if they would present at one of our sessions for three to five minutes. They could present on any topic, we just requested it be something that supported the other teachers in the room. They could share a lesson that worked well, a protocol that helped them, or how they use a particular application. These Light Bulb Talks became the heart of the cohort. They had a safe space to practice presenting using the new technology they were working with in their classroom, and they were sharing something they were proud of or had increased their expertise in.

For me, part of leadership is creating the structures and opportunities that allow others to lead. We need to create the space so people feel comfortable and welcome and valued.

We built this cohort to grow over three years. The first year focuses on the teacher shifting their classroom practice, the second year focuses on sharing their lessons beyond their school site and growing as a teacher leader, and the third year focuses on growing into a mentor for the next cohort.

I just completed my week of coaching, and it has been my favorite week of the school year so far. I went into all thirty classrooms of teachers who are participating in Cohort 1 and Cohort 2. To do this, I had to consider how to best organize my calendar and my days. I selected one week of the month as my cohort coaching week. I dedicated each day of that week to a specific school. Some months I had to bump a school up a week to accommodate a meeting, but mapping out that week in the month was key for my planning. I asked every teacher for their prep and created a list in my digital calendar. Ideally, I could visit the teacher for twenty to thirty minutes in the class prior to their prep and then stay with them to speak, reflect, support, and be a thought partner. My days were full, and full of joy and learning. I was there to witness teachers introducing video assignments, design challenges, vocabulary games, science notebooks, Socratic seminars, morning meetings, and much more.

The beauty in building this out over a dedicated week was that it helped me make connections across schools. During this time, a teacher said, "Thank you for sharing about that project in Mrs. L's classroom. I wish I could have been there to see it." *That's it! That is the next step for this group to grow as leaders.* They were asking for instructional rounds. This isn't a new concept, but the logistics were getting in their way. So, I removed that barrier. I had their schedules, so I created opt-in instructional rounds based around their prep periods.

I am proud that this group is now advocating for what they need to keep growing. They are true teacher leaders, building positive impact at their schools and throughout the district.

At a recent board meeting, a teacher summarized that impact with this profound statement: "I was ready to leave teaching after the pandemic, but this cohort brought back my joy. It was the best professional learning I have ever experienced. I grew, I feel more connected to my students, to my peers, and I feel inspired to keep learning and sharing and growing as a teacher leader."

This moment reminded me that it is a privilege to lead from this in-between space.

## Moving Forward

I have come to accept that my leadership journey rests in the in-between. It is continuous, it's OK if it changes, and it is OK if the path doesn't look the same as someone else's. I have been told that my position is a great stepping-stone. This may be true for some, but for me, I don't consider my role a stepping-stone. Instructional leadership coaching is meaningful on its own. I want to feel appreciated and valued in the present, and when I seek out encouragement on a next step, then I am ready to hear it. I feel lucky to have found trusted women leaders I can invite to lunch or text with. I use that time to vent and ask for advice. They often help me practice the way I want to share thoughts with a supervisor, and I'm grateful for the safety they provide me when I do. It is these women leaders who amplify my voice and encourage me to share. They help me to be a proud leader. I might not have a simple title to write on a name tag, but I know who I am. Nothing in life is simple, and that is OK.

### Actionable Ideas to Implement Tomorrow

- Help educators be seen and celebrated. Provide them a space to share about student learning. This can be by filming them, creating a podcast, or writing a blog or newsletter. Their words and reflections deserve sharing.
- Find space for others to give Light Bulb Talks and try giving one yourself. These can be done in a staff meeting, professional learning community (PLC), cohort, or other group setting.
- Find a trusted woman leader and ask her to go to lunch. Share with her what frustrates you, and also share what you are proud of. If you want advice, ask for it. If you need to celebrate, let her know.

CHAPTER FOUR

# From Teacher to Leader
## An Open Road Map of Advice

### BY LAUREN M. KAUFMAN

> *Leadership is a journey; you can't skip steps. You've got to show up and commit to the work every day.*
> —LINDA FAGAN

The influence of our teachers is indelibly woven into the fabric of our lives."[12] This is the opening to Julie Schmidt Hasson's book *Safe, Seen, and Stretched in the Classroom*.

As I packed up my family's belongings from a weekend trip, I listened to Sean Gaillard's *Principal Liner Notes* podcast where he highlighted Julie's book and her research around the impact of teachers. That inspiring conversation led me to read more of Julie's words. She goes on to ask, "Is there a teacher you remember? Not just the teacher's name, but specific things about him or her?"[13] I paused and thought deeply after reading those words. My answer is yes, there are many teachers who have left that magical, everlasting impact on my heart, provided me with sound advice and mentorship, and paved the way for the person I am and the person I strive to be.

I recognize that the **greatest teachers I have ever known hold a special kind of magic**. They take the time to see you as more than their student, but as a human being with the potential to make an impact on others in the future.

Over the course of my journey, I've crafted an eight-step road map to becoming just that kind of teacher. You'll find it at the end of this chapter.

## Family Roots in Education

Long before I encountered those teachers who influenced my life, I held the belief that teaching is an incredibly important job. This conviction was nurtured and shaped by the genuine guidance I received from my own family of educators. My Grandpa David was a law professor, and the walls of his home were adorned with shelves upon shelves of books he had authored or eagerly devoured, stacked floor to ceiling. As a little girl, I'd pull out the thick law textbooks he authored and thumb through the pages in awe of his knowledge and perseverance with writing. I wondered how he ever wrote so many important words on each page. I loved it when he challenged me to scavenger hunts, to find the names of his children, grandchildren, family, and friends that he'd used in the case studies outlined in his books. As I write this, I deeply wish he was still here so I could tell him that I have been writing consistently, that I, too, am now a published author. This is an accomplishment I never could have foreseen as I surveyed the sea of books that enveloped his dining room walls.

My Grandpa David adored teaching; I can vividly recall the fervor in his voice as he spoke about his students, his face brimming with pride. Countless little blue composition booklets were wildly stacked around his office, bearing testimony to his dedication and passion for his students. He delighted in entertaining our family with anecdotes about them, ensuring his love for teaching was instilled within our hearts. Immersed in his students' written assignments, he dedicated hours upon hours to provide them with meticulous feedback. His purpose was clear: to unlock their potential, encourage them to become reflective thinkers, and cultivate fresh ideas that could bring about positive change in the world. "Lauren, you should see how wonderful my students are," he would exclaim with smiling eyes.

As a teenager, I had the privilege of accompanying my Grandpa David to work. There, I witnessed these extraordinary interactions firsthand. It was not a regular sight for me to witness my grandpa unleashing his humorous side in the classroom, but it was through his students' laughter that I knew how much they adored him. While I didn't yet know that my own destiny lay in the realm of education, I did know that I aspired to follow in the footsteps of my Grandpa David.

My parents were also beloved teachers in the community where I grew up; my dad an English teacher, and my mom a special education and reading teacher. From childhood into adulthood, I observed them spending countless hours building connections with students, families, and colleagues, reading student papers, providing meaningful feedback, and creating engaging lessons. I can't remember a day in public without students rushing toward them to spark conversations rooted in stories of gratitude and appreciation for the legacy they left behind. "You were the best teacher I have ever known!" and "You helped me realize who I needed and wanted to be" or just a simple "Thank you for everything." My sister, Brooke, is also an educator. Since I didn't pursue education right after college (I was in the field of cosmetics, a WHOLE other story), she took the time to coach me with sound advice as I applied for my first teaching positions, carefully looking over my demonstration lesson plans and preparing me for interviews. The passion she has for teaching, learning, and student success is palpable. Can you imagine the dialogue that happens when we're all in the same room together? When we are not together, my dad shares the latest educational articles on a family text thread, supporting our growth as parents and educators.

I left the classroom many years ago, and to this day, I can still feel the grief and emptiness of not having students to call my own. It's the kind of feeling that makes your heart pound and twists your stomach into knots. The thought of not being my students' number one still makes me sad. I always viewed the classroom as the epicenter of relationships, learning, growth, and transformation. Each classroom within a school community is a special haven bubbling with curiosity, wonder, and joyful learning. Each one is filled with its own special stories and inside jokes. Every class is made up of a network of unique personalities. Being a classroom teacher can be hard. It can be stressful. It can be emotionally draining. The responsibility can just be exhausting. But, after many years in education and having served in different roles, I am certain that the classroom is one of the most magical places on earth!

## The Legacy We Leave Behind

I often think about my former students. I wonder where they are, what they are doing, if they are happy, and whether or not they are pursuing their dreams. I perseverate over whether they took something they learned with me into the real world. I love sharing stories about my classroom days with my colleagues, with students in the classrooms I visit, and through my writing. My work becomes more meaningful when I can make and share connections to it.

A few years ago, in the midst of answering work emails, I heard the *ping* of another email reach my inbox. I had to blink a few times and go through my mental filing cabinet to connect the sender's name with the sentiments expressed inside. I realized that it was from a former second-grade student who was in my class ten years prior.

The email read as follows:

> *Hey Mrs. Kaufman!*
>
> *I just wanted to let you know that I have officially enrolled at a university, with a major in computer science/game design. I want to thank you for all the love and support all these years, it means the world to me. I was hoping to have a big graduation*

> party and seeing you there, but alas, I haven't left the house in two months due to COVID-19 and that probably won't change anytime soon. I hope all is well with you and the family! Thanks again for everything, and I hope to see you soon.
>
> Thanks a bunch,
> Ben

Oh yes, it was Ben—how could I forget him? Inquisitive, kind, collaborative, confident, funny, joyful. Not to mention, he was an avid reader who knew where every single book in the classroom library belonged, even with his eyes closed! He could give you a detailed summary of any book he read using the most descriptive language and sophisticated vocabulary. He loved to chat with his friends, even when he was supposed to be listening to a lesson, but it didn't bother me; it made me love him more. When he had a thought or idea, he would impulsively blurt it out to me, to his classmates—whomever would listen!

I remember his mom coming into the classroom to help me plan wonderful learning experiences for the children. She had a special way of empowering me as a new teacher, welcoming me into a new school community, and making me feel at ease when I was missing my newborn baby like crazy (only two and a half months old at the time). Ben's mom kept in touch with me for years, sending me holiday cards, updates about Ben, their family and pets, even funny quotes and well wishes. She would genuinely ask me about how my family and I were doing, "just because." Years later, when she heard that my community and my home had been devastated in Hurricane Sandy, she generously offered my family her apartment after we lost our home. Her belief in me created a special connection that will always be cherished.

When I entered education, it was never my first intent to earn a satisfactory observation report or get recognition from anyone else. My priority was to be a learner, a connector, a bridge that unites relationships to learning. Emails like Ben's serve as a reminder of why I wanted to be in education in the first place.

It is the footprints you leave in students' hearts that cannot be quantified or measured in a single snapshot observation, conversation, or moment in time. Relationships cannot be encapsulated solely by the curriculum you teach, the assessments you administer, or the projects you assign. Be magical! The footprints you leave will be eternally imprinted in your heart as well as theirs.

## From Teacher to Leader

In my transition from teacher to administrator, I questioned if I could leave a lasting impact and be the transformative leader I aspired to be. Regardless of our roles, we must show up and realize that perfection is unattainable. It's our imperfections that shape us as leaders.

In Adam Grant's *ReThinking* podcast, Admiral Linda Fagan, commandant of the US Coast Guard, emphasized the need to break through the walls of insulation as a leader.[14] Walls can form if we're not intentional in our approach. Always remember that you were chosen to share spaces with educators and students, and it's in embracing our own imperfections that we break through those walls and become the leaders we are meant to be.

When you first became an educator, were you handed a road map to transformational success? Have you thought about the advice you'd offer a first-year teacher or administrator? In those early years of teaching and leading, I believed a magical handbook would be waiting for my arrival, revealing the perfect recipe for becoming a successful educator and leader. Well, that day never came because such a handbook doesn't exist.

Even after years of schooling, internships, teaching, leadership adventures, extensive reading, and podcast listening, I understand that nothing prepares educators and leaders for new roles like diving into the trenches with people as guides. From my viewpoint, every person in an educational organization is a leader for kids. I'm sure anyone who has led their own classroom, a school building, or an entire district understands the tremendous responsibility, both gratifying and overwhelming, that comes with it.

Whether you're a teacher or an administrator, those in a position to influence children's lives recognize the unique opportunity to leave an everlasting impact. Gifts live within exceptional educators, waiting to be unwrapped in the right place, at the right time, with the right people. They can't be found in any handbook or road map because education and learning have no fixed rules and no endpoint. As Simon Sinek, author of *The Infinite Game*, explains, education is an infinite game without a finish line, with players, curricula, policies, and procedures that continually evolve.[15]

*So, who is it that crafts the invisible road map to success?*

While I had formal mentors as a new teacher and administrator, I've been fortunate to consider many educators as mentors throughout my career. They have shared words of wisdom, resources, and new ideas that have influenced the way I approach transformational leadership forever. In fact, I perceive every single educator I have ever met, since the beginning of my career, to be a mentor. Why is that? Some have gifted me with advice I will always hold close, while others have modeled practices that I would never even consider employing. I have taken all the wisdom shared with me over the years and created my own open road map to share with you for consideration. It includes eight pieces of advice for new teachers and leaders!

## Actionable Ideas to Implement Tomorrow

I call this an "open road map" of advice because these are only suggestions, a framework, a guide. These are signposts to point any new educator and leader in the right direction, but it is up to you to choose your path and decide what kind of educator and leader you want to be.

My hope is that this open road map of advice finds its way into the hands of mentors dedicated to nurturing strong foundations for educators, as well as new teachers who embrace lifelong learning as a journey. May these eight pieces of advice serve as an inspiration to imagine what the future could hold for you, and for the people you will continue to influence throughout your career.

**8 PIECES OF ADVICE FOR EDUCATORS AND LEADERS**

- Keep Connections at the Core
- Embrace the Community
- Build a Network
- Discover & Document
- Pursue Professional Learning
- Be a Mirror
- Celebrate Success & Invite Failure
- Pause & Reflect

LAURENMKAUFMAN.COM | @LAURENMKAUFMAN

- **Keep Connections at the Core:** Get to know your students, colleagues, families, and communities by listening to their stories, passions, and interests; this intentional action will show them that you are human first and that you care. Be that person who wears an empathy lens. Be someone who takes the time to walk in the shoes of every student and colleague who crosses your path. By creating those connections and cultivating meaningful relationships, you open pathways to deeper learning and exponential growth! Jim Knight encapsulates this approach in his ASCD article, "Seven Principles for True Partnership," where he describes his role in educational environments: "Instead of telling teachers what they should do, I saw myself as a facilitator creating the conditions for dialogue. Instead of seeing myself as an expert, I saw myself as a partner."[16] This philosophy is at the heart of how I engage with others, utilizing

Knight's Seven Partnership Principles to ground conversations and foster connections. The principles as defined in the ASCD article are:

1. **Equality:** I don't believe any person or group is more valuable than any other. I recognize and honor the dignity of every individual.
2. **Choice:** I communicate in a way that acknowledges the professional discretion of others by positioning them as decision makers.
3. **Voice:** I want to hear what others have to say, and I communicate that clearly.
4. **Dialogue:** I believe conversations should consist of a back-and-forth exchange, with all parties hearing and responding to one another's opinions.
5. **Reflection:** I engage in conversations that look back, look at, and look ahead.
6. **Praxis:** I structure learning so that it's grounded in real life.
7. **Reciprocity:** I enter each conversation open and expecting to learn.

- **Embrace the Community:** Make an effort to learn the mission and vision at the community, district, and building levels. Those who make up the culture and climate of your organization are rowing in the same direction to best serve the students! Every role in an organization is important and should be valued. You are now part of a team, and it takes a village to provide students with the right opportunities to thrive. You do not have to work in isolation. Observe and talk with the people around you; you will be surprised at how much you learn from them. Those conversations will stretch your thinking and have an immediate impact on your role. You will also gain a better understanding of who you can turn to for direction and advice when you need it!
- **Build a Network:** Although an outstanding formal mentor is crucial to the growth process, it is vital to connect and collaborate with other educators and staff members in your educational communities.

Everyone has knowledge and gifts to share. We are truly better together. Try not to compare yourself to others. According to Theodore Roosevelt, "Comparison is the thief of joy." We are not here to compete. We are here for the kids! Just like we have different friends for various reasons (those who make us laugh, give us advice, listen to understand, or talk so we don't have to), the same holds true for the educators we meet. Find the people in your organization who can make you better and help you see and learn other practices and perspectives. Also, consider expanding your network by using social media platforms. That's how I have met some of the most impactful people to push my thinking in ways I never knew they could. Some have also become great friends!

- **Discover and Document:** One of the best opportunities I was afforded was the chance to watch great teachers teach and great leaders lead! Intervisitations, lab sites, and debriefing time will allow you to discover and embed new practices into your repertoire of teaching and learning tools! If this doesn't happen in your school district, ask! Perhaps your administrators can arrange for it (even virtually). If you are lucky enough to have instructional coaches, ask them to organize this authentic learning experience, but also invite them to come in and offer constructive feedback. I always loved when my coaches and peers gave me new ideas. They encouraged me to try new approaches and made me better! You may also consider creating a digital portfolio, which allows you to document and think about your learning in intentional and meaningful ways. I am grateful to George Couros for encouraging me to start mine just a few years ago. Luckily, I took his incredible Digital Portfolio Master Course, in which he walked me through the purpose and process of creating and using one.[17] The experience has been reflective and allows me to create a digital footprint of my own learning. It's never too late to start. Don't think too hard about it. Just jump right in and make it happen—you won't be sorry!

- **Pursue Professional Learning:** I have been fortunate to work in school districts that provide professional learning opportunities for all leaders and teachers. These districts see the value in offering a range of courses that fit with the district's mission and vision while meeting the needs of the staff and students. To me, the most impactful leaders empower and elevate teachers and leaders within the district by bringing in great educators and thought leaders from outside the organization to facilitate targeted professional learning experiences. These experiences have ensured that I can provide appropriate, relevant, and innovative professional learning for new teachers and leaders. I am also a big believer in not waiting for your district to provide professional learning for you. I REPEAT: do not wait! If there is something out there that will help meet the needs of your learners (and you) then pursue it and find it! Then, ask if you can attend it! Social media has been a space to professionally grow, and it's FREE! Consider joining an X chat that is rooted in a topic you are interested in! Read professional books, articles and blog posts, and listen to podcasts. Elisabeth Bostwick and I recommended a plethora of inspiring podcasts in an Edutopia article we cowrote titled "Making Podcasts Part of Professional Learning."[18] In another Edutopia article I cowrote with Stephanie Rothstein, "Taking Control of Your Professional Growth,"[19] we share some of our favorite professional learning resources. Also, if you are having difficulty finding a professional learning opportunity that meets your needs, then consider CREATING IT. You should always be in the driver's seat of your learning!
- **Be a Mirror:** Think about all the educators and leaders who have influenced your practice. You may not have even met some of them yet! Think about *why* those people were an important part of your journey. What did they *say* or *do* to influence the choices you make daily? Take the best qualities of those educators, mirror those attributes, and make them your own! If possible, reach out to them and tell them exactly *why* and *how* they have inspired you. They will be

happy to hear it! Sometimes, we don't recognize the impact we are having in the moment. Be the mirror and reflect the best versions of all those people!

- **Celebrate Successes and Failures:** It is crucial to give yourself recognition for all successes, big and small. You are doing hard work, and you should be able to share your amazing moments of growth and awe with those who support and cheer you on! There is nothing more gratifying than knowing you have made a difference in the lives of your students and colleagues. At the same time, when you enter the field of education, you must be prepared to fail many times throughout your career. *THIS IS A GOOD THING.* I repeat: *THIS IS A GOOD THING.* When you aren't failing, it means that you are not trying new things. It means that you may not be pushing yourself outside your comfort zone. So celebrate success AND failure. You've earned it!

- **Pause and Reflect:** Educators and leaders work hard and exhaust every minute in their precious days. Great educators and leaders also have servant hearts and are usually thinking about everyone else's needs but their own. Take the time to pause and reflect. That means, take a break! Pursue your personal passions and interests, and practice self-care in the best way it suits you. This will look different for everyone. Some will indulge in their favorite exercise routines or go on a shopping spree. Others will take a painting class, read for pleasure, and/or write a book like me! The point is, whatever makes you happy on the inside, whatever pleasures your heart, do it! Taking those breaks to focus on YOU will make you a better educator than you were before!

## PART II

# Mentors Are All Around Us

CHAPTER FIVE

# Mentorship Matters

## BY LAUREN M. KAUFMAN

> *Mentoring is a two-way street, and the mentor benefits as much as the mentee. When I see the progress and success of those I have mentored, I am immensely proud.*
>
> —SHERYL SANDBERG

Adversity can lead you in the right direction, opening new paths. Opportunities can live inside obstacles. The setbacks and obstacles you face are not the sum total of your life; they are mere moments of discomfort that bridge your past to your future. So, as you continue carving your own path on the journey to leadership, let these opportunities serve as mentors and guides.

Every year, school districts around the world entrust thousands of new educators to serve their communities as they hire and provide them with a special opportunity to begin long, meaningful educational careers. Most likely, these educators have endured rigorous processes to determine that they can make an unmistakable and everlasting impact on the lives of the world's most precious gift—children. Make no mistake, when someone makes a commitment to becoming an educator, they assume a tremendous responsibility. They will create pathways of promise with the power to influence learners for the rest of their lives.

Teaching is not just something you do; it's a calling. It's a beautiful gift, an opportunity to unleash the talents within every human being you encounter. It's also a time to cultivate powerful relationships that can stand the test of time. Teaching and leading create a space to collaborate with colleagues and build bridges to connect previous learning to new and innovative ideas. Educators and leaders are responsible for shaping significant moments that can leave profound imprints in the hearts and minds of every learner and colleague they meet. Teaching and leading is also hard work. It can be extremely emotional. It can be draining. But, it's so incredibly rewarding.

As a leader, *how will you leverage your experiences to serve as a mentor for your colleagues, staff, and students, fostering their personal and professional growth in a way that leaves a lasting impact on their journey?* One phrase that comes to mind: *mentorship matters!*

## Embracing Leadership Opportunities

The journey to becoming a great educator and leader is an ongoing process of self-discovery and growth. The mentors placed in your path have played a crucial role in helping you bring out the best version of yourself. As you continue to discover the leader that lives inside you, you may recognize the significant influence your mentors have had on the leader you are becoming.

As you navigate your career, keep your eyes open to the new opportunities emerging before you. They have the potential to naturally build capacity in you, and to elevate others. It's exciting to think about the people you haven't met yet. They will make vital contributions to your growth and shape the leader you strive to become, and they await your arrival at your next destination because you were meant to be there. In Brené Brown's *Dare to Lead* podcast, Simon Sinek shares, "Faith is knowing that you're on a team, even if you don't know who the players are."[20] Consider every moment on your journey as a significant step toward your future. When you approach every observation and interaction as a learning experience, you enhance your leadership lens and embrace new opportunities that nurture your talents in unanticipated times and places.

In his best-selling book *Atomic Habits*, James Clear shares that "every action we take is like a vote for the type of person you wish to become."[21] When you are striving to be your personal best, you step out of your comfort zone and explore other opportunities a little more deeply. Leaps of faith invite a range of emotions. From joy to excitement, to wish fulfillment and disappointment. Yes, disappointment. In *Atlas of the Heart*, Brené Brown defines this uncomfortable feeling: "Disappointment is unmet expectations. The more significant the expectations, the more significant the disappointment." At every level of an organization, leaders will come face-to-face with rejection and obstacles. Chances are, you'll encounter times where your expectations don't align with other people's visions as you work to implement new ideas. Brown goes on to share, "When we develop expectations, we paint a picture in our head of how things are going to be, and how they're going to look."[22]

As an educator and leader, many outcomes are beyond our control. There is a gap between what we want to see and what actually happens. While we may have high hopes for the outcomes of our efforts, it is important to acknowledge that external barriers can get in the way. For example, how other people think, what they feel, and their judgments and perceptions of you might not reflect your intent, true purpose, who you are, and who you continually strive to be. The road to and through leadership can feel daunting. Reaching for leadership opportunities by putting yourself out there to the world can leave you feeling vulnerable. There will be moments when you're determined to make a vision a reality, achieve specific goals, or explore new ideas. During these times, it's common to create stories in our minds about how things should unfold. However, many of these narratives are purely imagined and don't reflect reality.

For example, when you commit to the interview process, you are accepting everything it involves, including the preparation, learning, nerves, critical and constructive feedback, and possible setbacks. Remember that you don't have to go through this process alone. As I mentioned earlier, my mentor Linda Roth helped me through my own processes. She was a great source of inspiration and support as I endured rejections throughout my leadership search. I encourage aspiring leaders to seek out similar support systems as you navigate your own journey toward leadership. I have no doubt that you will overcome any obstacles with a mentor who fills your soul with reassurance and the confidence you need to persevere through the process.

In the midst of completing my leadership credential, I wasn't sure when would be the right time to explore opportunities and start applying for administrative positions. I didn't even realize that sometimes people get "tapped on the shoulder" to apply for these roles. Those taps can happen when you least expect it! While weighing my options, I was unexpectedly tapped on the shoulder for two very different administrative roles. One was an assistant principal position in an elementary school, a role that was right in my wheelhouse, and the other was an assistant principal in a middle school, which was definitely out of my comfort zone.

Simultaneously, another intriguing leadership opportunity was posted in my district, the role of mentor coordinator K–12. Although this was not an administrative role, I viewed it as an opportunity to develop a mentor program that would build a strong foundation for teachers to have long, meaningful careers with strong networks of support. The thought of inspiring teachers toward a positive career trajectory sounded exhilarating. Although I was not tapped on the shoulder for this role, it did not discourage me from applying! In retrospect, I can still feel myself grappling with the decision about whether to stick to what I knew or take a leap of faith. In *She Leads: The Women's Guide to a Career in Educational Leadership* by Dr. Rachel George and Majalise W. Tolan, they share the following empowering sentiment: "You never know what job you can have, what you need to do to improve, or how badly you want something until you apply. Let's go!"[23] Ultimately, I decided to go for all three opportunities. I figured, why not? The worst that could happen was that I wouldn't get any of the positions!

The afternoon I had a screening interview for the middle school assistant principal position happened to be the same day I was helping an elementary school facilitate activity rotations during a school-wide Activity Day event. In the weeks leading up to that interview, I had done my research about the school, read a few great books including *The Assistant Principal 50* by Baruti K. Kafele, *The Innovator's Mindset* by George Couros, and *Dare to Lead* by Brené Brown. I had reached out to mentors, administrators who served as assistant principals, and talked through many scenarios. I felt as ready as I could be for a position that seemed out of my reach. But, I did receive a "tap," so I thought there was a chance for me.

When I got to work, I retrieved the schedule that listed which rotation I would supervise during Activity Day. Do you want to know what it said? "Lauren Kaufman—THE BOUNCY HOUSE!" Anyone who knows what a bouncy house filled with kids looks like on Activity Day understands that this is an extremely stressful job. You're basically keeping kids from crushing each other the entire time. I remember thinking this assignment would not allow me to mentally prepare for this interview, leaving me a bit stressed. On the other hand, I wouldn't have to think about it anymore or perseverate over it.

When the school day was over, I rushed home, freshened up, threw on a professional suit, and made it to the interview a few minutes early. When I was finally called into the room, I realized that the interview was over before it began. After a quick scan of the room, I saw that one important seat at the table was empty: a key person who made the hiring decisions. Then I took a quick read of the others who sat at the shiny lacquered wooden oval table before me. I studied their faces, their body language, and the overall feeling that permeated the room. A sinking feeling pushed on my heart. Many people may not know this about me, but I consider myself to be a pretty intuitive person. This gift is truly a blessing and a curse. I get strong feelings about people and circumstances before they happen, and I am left with lingering, hard to explain feelings after the interactions have passed. So, I made the quick decision to show up anyway and give the interview all I had, although it was clear to my intuition that I didn't have a chance. After that interview, I didn't hear anything for quite some time, but I already knew the outcome. So, it was no surprise that when the call did come, I was relieved that the "we regret to inform you" courtesy conversation, along with the courtesy interview, were behind me.

So, what happened with the elementary assistant principal role I was "tapped" for? Well, I went through four rounds of interviews and endured a rigorous process. It came down to one other person and me. Do you want to guess the outcome of that rigorous experience filled with several interview rounds? Yes, you probably guessed it—I didn't get that job, either. Full transparency, the double disappointment really crushed my spirit. I questioned everything about myself, from my abilities, to my core values, to my purpose. I also reflected on the infamous taps on the shoulder and came to the realization that these taps were genuine. They were. I don't think anyone would go out of their way to tell you to apply for a position unless they felt you were capable and would be an asset to their organization. However, knowing what I know now, there are layers of other factors involved in hiring, different perspectives brought to the table, and as my former mentor Principal Mrs. Karen Sauter would say, the "invisible strings" we cannot see during the process.

After some time, I pushed through the hurt and disappointment, picked my head up, and told myself that those jobs just weren't supposed to be mine. As my friend, author, and educational leader Meghan Lawson would say, "Nothing that is for you will miss you." The universe had a better plan for me, and the people I was destined to meet needed me in another place, at the right time. I would later use the lessons learned from these experiences to better myself for other opportunities on the horizon. Ryan Holiday's sentiment in his book *The Obstacle Is the Way* reaffirms this feeling: "Yes, because obstacles are actually opportunities to test ourselves, to try new things, and ultimately, to triumph. The obstacle is the way."[24]

Shortly after hearing the news, I made some phone calls and sent some text messages to my references and a few other close friends and mentors. After I hit Send on the last text message, I felt relieved that I could put those experiences behind me and reach for the ones that were waiting. It was a moment of respite amid the storm of disappointment. However, just as I began to settle into that sense of relief, another phone call lit up my smartphone screen. I cautiously picked it up as I was not in the mood to have a conversation.

"Hi Lauren, I thought you did a really great job on the interview for the mentor coordinator, and I would love to offer you the position!" My goodness, I'll admit, amid the negative self-talk renting space in my head over the fresh disappointments, I had not considered that I'd interviewed for the mentor coordinator position in my own school district.

"Oh, really? Wow, yes. I would love the opportunity. Yes. Thank you so much. I'm looking forward to it," I responded with a new outlook, ready to walk toward a new path and challenge that would later open doors I could have never imagined.

Regardless of the outcome, let every experience you endure on your path reveal something significant about who you are meant to be. In my own personal journey, I discovered I was meant to exemplify why mentorship matters to other educators. This realization ultimately led to an incredible opportunity to lead something special, cultivate new connections, and acquire new knowledge that would shape me as a leader for years to come. By embracing the idea of mentorship and sharing my own experiences, I could leave an infinite impact on the lives of others while growing into the leader I was becoming.

## Actionable Ideas to Implement Tomorrow

### Questions Aspiring Leaders Can Think about and Learn From

**Invite Leadership Opportunities:**
- How can you actively seek out new opportunities for growth and leadership in your current role or organization?
- What steps can you take to step out of your comfort zone and embrace new challenges and collaborations?

**Manage Expectations and Disappointment:**
- How can you approach disappointment and setbacks as opportunities for growth and learning?
- What specific techniques or mindsets can you adopt to help you navigate disappointment more effectively?

**Seek Support Systems:**
- Who are the individuals in your life that can serve as mentors, colleagues, or friends to support your leadership journey?
- In what ways can you contribute to creating a supportive environment for others who are aspiring leaders?

**Embrace Obstacles as Opportunities:**
- How can you shift your mindset to view obstacles as opportunities for growth and personal transformation?
- What specific strategies or techniques can you use to reframe challenges in a positive light?

**Reflect and Learn from Experiences:**
- What are some methods or practices you can implement to regularly reflect on your experiences as a leader?
- How can you extract lessons from both positive and negative experiences to enhance your leadership skills and personal growth?

CHAPTER SIX

# Stepping into Leadership

## BY LAUREN M. KAUFMAN

*Rarely are opportunities presented to you in a perfect way. In a nice little box with a yellow bow on top. "Here, open it, it's perfect. You'll love it." Opportunities—the good ones—are messy, confusing, and hard to recognize. They're risky. They challenge you.*

—SUSAN WOJCICKI

## The Opportunity that Opened Doors

One of my greatest opportunities was being entrusted to facilitate the mentor program in my previous school district. It allowed me to lay a strong foundation for educators and guide them on the path to long, fulfilling careers, and I could highlight the gratifying, essential role of educators in shaping the leaders of today and tomorrow. This special experience allowed me to help teachers build self-efficacy and ownership, and impart the truth: educators need one other to truly make a difference. That is why developing a strong mentor program has one of the highest returns on investment in the world of education.

When I stepped into this role, I was given autonomy to figure out the leader I was destined to become and embody the one I always needed. There were no parameters, no handbook to guide the direction

I would take. Drawing from the wisdom of mentors throughout my career, I understood that as an aspiring leader, I couldn't rely solely on others to initiate the ideas I wanted to bring to life. I had to take the initiative and make them happen. By aligning with the vision rooted in my school district's priorities, grounding the work in the state's mentoring standards, and incorporating my own experiences and the insights of others, I was able to create a meaningful blueprint for the present and the future.

I approached this role with a deep sense of gratitude, determined to give the mentor program all I had to offer. Since I was empowered to lead the program with autonomy and to shape the framework and messaging, I chose to introduce innovative opportunities that would help teachers recognize the gifts inside themselves. My goal was to empower them to develop agency, prioritize relationships, and lead with sound minds and hearts.

Mentorship matters on so many levels. The creation of powerful professional learning communities fosters the next generation of teacher leaders and helps educators see the value of being in a constant state of learning and transformation. According to the New York State Mentoring Standards, "The purpose of *NYS Program Guidance and Standards for Mentoring* is to offer program guidance and a set of standards to build a system of supports to retain and help new educators thrive in their local context and the profession . . . Mentoring helps new teachers make necessary connections between educational theory and practice and supports their professional and personal growth. For the mentor teacher, mentoring enables professional development/learning opportunities and connections with colleagues. These opportunities establish a relationship where the new teacher is connected and supported within their local organization."[25] Establishing and implementing a strong mentor program enables novice teachers to be guided by mentors, and helps learners reach their maximum social-emotional, cognitive, and academic growth throughout their school years and beyond. This distinguished responsibility empowers more experienced educators to take everything they have learned and "pay it forward" to help new teachers acclimate to the culture and climate of an organization, shatter the walls of isolation during the inception of their careers, and shape the next generation of teacher leaders.

## Pursuing the Vision

In pursuit of this vision, I dove into a book that embodied my aspirations—*The Innovator's Mindset* by George Couros. George is a renowned learner, speaker, author, and innovative leader in the field of education. Little did I know that this book would serve as a compass in my future as a lead learner and writer. In one of George's best-known sentiments, he states, "Change is an opportunity to do something amazing."[26] It was through George's profound insights that I began to step out of my comfort zone and shape my understanding of leadership and educational impact. Reaching out to George allowed me to connect him with both the new and veteran educators I was mentoring. He always graciously responded, sending video messages and even virtually meeting with us. It was in those moments that I realized George's belief in my potential, even when I doubted myself.

By embracing the 8 Characteristics of the Innovator's Mindset and connecting with George during the mentor program, I found my own voice.

I shared my insights through my blog and embraced the opportunity to work toward writing this book. Reflecting on this incredible journey, I firmly believe that the leader I have become today, constantly evolving, relentlessly striving, and devoted to making a profound impact on the lives of educators and students, would not have been possible without the experience of stepping into mentorship. It is a leadership role that I will always hold close to my heart.

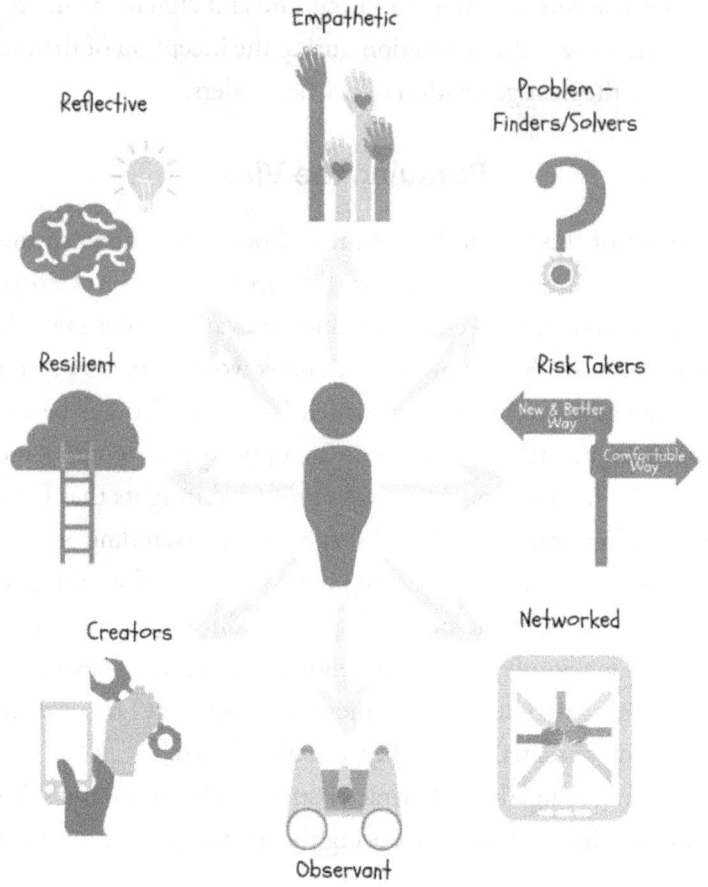

Some may perceive each role you serve in over the course of your career as a stepping-stone to get to the next. I don't. I believe the roles you fulfill are more than stepping-stones; they are mirrors that reflect your evolution as a practitioner. The learning and development you experience over time strengthens and sharpens your empathetic and instructional lenses, allowing you to better serve others.

I read the following quote on X from George and immediately pasted it into the notes section of my phone (a space where I keep quotes, ideas, and inspiration): "Many leaders are scared about developing people and then having them leave. They should be more worried about not developing people and having them stay." I read it several times, and then I read it some more.

Something about the sentiment resonated with me. Could it be that I had left a school district where I thought I would retire to embark instead on an educational journey as a school leader? Could it be that I've served in many roles throughout my career, and the quote made me think about all the educators who motivated me to take risks, try new things, and share my learning and gifts with others, while helping to pave the way to advocate for my personal and professional growth? Was it these leaders' ability to clearly communicate a vision and develop that vision with their staff and students? Was it that these exceptional leaders included all the appropriate stakeholders in the decision-making process instead of having a few people "in the room where it happens"?

Perhaps these words encouraged me to reflect on the qualities those inspiring leaders possessed to help mentor, support, and guide me and others to a new and better direction. Or their ability to foster relationships within their school community by ensuring everyone felt invited and welcomed. Maybe it was the strong instructional lens that enabled them to be viewed as credible instructional leaders who had a firm grasp on teaching and learning and could teach students and staff at any given time. Was it their ability to leave their ego at the door by focusing on people, not titles, putting trust in others, and continuously building capacity from within? I've encountered all of these attributes of great leaders, and those who have served as mentors have contributed to the leaps of faith I have taken throughout my career.

Here are some more of my observations about leaders who develop leaders. They:

- Optimize, not criticize.
- Give recognition.
- Show sincere appreciation.
- Value other perspectives.

- Show humility, vulnerability, and talk about their own mistakes.
- Ask questions and make suggestions.
- Celebrate big and small wins.
- Give honest feedback.

In *Lead from Where You Are: Building Intention, Connection, and Direction in Our Schools,* Dr. Joe Sanfelippo shares, "Finding those who push your thinking and support you in the journey is key to moving forward—and transforming your school community into a group of potential leaders."[27] Joe is right. There are those you meet along the way who become a vital part of your team. Whether they come into your life for a few moments, a few hours, a few days, weeks, or years, these people can make a profound impact on your growth and development as a professional and human being. They see something in you; they perceive the spark that ignites ideas. They've witnessed your ability to change the trajectory of the lives of others. They see that you can rally people together to create meaningful change. They see your positive spirit, your ability to listen to understand, and your action-oriented approach to creation and innovation.

Great leaders view themselves as thought partners as you navigate the ebb and flow of an ever-changing educational landscape. They help you row in the right direction while keeping kids at the core of the journey. Dr. Sanfelippo brilliantly raised the following reflective questions: "The question is not, are you going to be remembered as the leader in your space? The question is, how are you going to be remembered as the leader in your space?"[28] So I ask you, what type of leader do you want to be? If you commit to recognizing the gifts in others and see the value they bring to your organization, will you give them wings and let them fly? When I served as the mentor coordinator, I was determined to give new teachers their wings early on in their careers, lifting them up and giving them permission to find the leader inside as they were flying and trying new and innovative things.

A few years ago, I was packing up personal items from my assistant principal's office and preparing for my new role as the director of literacy. My mind relived the advice I'd received from mentors, the lessons I had learned from each role I'd served in, and the advice I would have given my first-year teacher self if I had gone through the mentor program I later created. As I was wrapped up in my past, I thought about the book *Because of a Teacher Volume II*, written and curated by George Couros, and the sentiment he shared: "Looking back is the key to moving forward."[29] Taking with me all I had learned, especially as I embraced the importance of mentorship, I couldn't agree more. Looking back is an opportunity to approach every endeavor with the strength and courage you will need to embrace a new journey. You can relive your collection of experiences and embrace them as more than stepping-stones; they are the bridges you built to lead you to the new beginnings that await on the horizon.

## Actionable Ideas to Implement Tomorrow

Developing a strong mentor program will create a foundation that sets educators on the right trajectory. If implemented with intention and purpose, they will develop and grow into the next generation of teacher leaders. These leaders have the potential to broaden their impact and expand their influence by stepping into formal leadership roles and paying it forward by creating more leaders. These ideas were born out of an opportunity to lead and facilitate a mentor program in a previous school district, and I carry them with me in the leadership roles I serve in today.

### Eight Tips for Developing a Strong Mentor Program

- **Align with state mentoring standards:** It is paramount to refer to the mentoring standards provided by the state/country you reside in. These standards are critical to teacher induction and to the design and implementation of relevant and meaningful learning experiences.

This enables the mentor coordinator to establish systemic efforts that will shape and sustain the first experiences in the careers of new teachers.

- **Voice and Choice:** It is vital to include educators in the decision-making process to share what kinds of professional learning they want to experience. It is also critical to recognize that educators enter the teaching profession with many strengths and areas for growth. The mentor coordinator needs to ensure that professional learning choices are grounded in the vision and mission of their school district. As an example, providing educators with a Google Form with a list of choices as well as a space to add any additional thoughts/ideas for professional growth will empower them to take ownership over their learning.
- **Professional Learning Communities:** By establishing a learner-centered culture of trust, connection, communication, and collaboration, educators have a valuable opportunity. They come to see the value in collectively setting reasonable, learner-driven, evidence-informed goals. They get to share ideas of instructional practice that will benefit ALL learners in their organizations. Not only will this improve skills, expertise, and knowledge through professional dialogue, but it will foster a desire to improve educational aspirations and achievement. This cultivates the next generation of teacher leaders. These teacher leaders will become an integral part of a cycle that improves and encourages innovative teaching and learning practices.
- **Select a Professional Book as a Framework:** One of the most valuable practices in a strong mentor program is using timeless professional books by outstanding authors who share their authentic experiences as educators at different levels of an organization. These books encompass innovative and relevant messages that stand the test of time regardless of what transpires in education. Take a deep dive into these books and be sure to connect the authors' messages with your district's mission and vision. These books will serve as

frameworks to drive the learning process. The books I intentionally chose are *The Innovator's Mindset* by George Couros and *Personal and Authentic* by Thomas C. Murray. Both authors share incredible resources and have been continuously accessible to new teachers, their mentors, and me. This has supported our efforts to keep learners at the heart of decision-making and able to implement lifelong practices that prepare them for any path they choose.

- **Invite Other Voices:** It is crucial to highlight the educators within your organization to facilitate professional learning experiences. This gives new teachers opportunities to connect with other educators across the school district, but also elevates the teacher leaders and administrators who can share knowledge and best teaching and learning practices with your educational community. Additionally, you will want to invite educators/speakers outside of your school district who can offer a fresh perspective on various topics in education. Those voices are also valuable as they have seen the work of other school districts around the world and can share a lens that can push your thinking outside of your comfort zone!

- **Create a Digital Footprint:** I have always stressed the importance of making your learning visible by sharing best teaching and learning practices with colleagues in your organization and beyond. By creating a mentor program hashtag and X handle, this allows participants in the program to showcase the incredible work within their learning spaces to a larger community. This will in turn help other educators create and form ideas that will ultimately benefit all learners! Feel free to check out the #LBLeads and @LBMentorProgram hashtag I created for the mentor program I facilitated.

- **Connected and Networked:** In *The Innovator's Mindset*, George Couros says, "Being in spaces where people actively share ideas makes us smarter."[30] Social media provides a space to connect with other educators who share our mindsets, but also pushes our thinking to create new and better ideas. It is in these spaces that we can get inspiration from other educators and organizations outside of education to try something new. Creating a culture of learning and innovation happens when meaningful connections are made beyond the walls of our own organizations. New possibilities are discovered within these spaces to benefit learners who have the potential to make change today and in the future!

- **Give Recognition:** Everyone in an educational organization works tirelessly to meet the needs of their learners. New teachers are acclimating to the culture and climate of a district, learning to understand their community, building new relationships, and learning new standards and a new curriculum, all while meeting the needs of families and students. They deserve all the recognition in the world! Celebrate your teacher leaders. It is human nature to want to feel valued and recognized. At mentor meetings, highlight the work they have been doing by looking through the hashtag you created and put those posts on a few slides! Have them explain the "why" behind their practices. For the educators who are not on social media, have them send pictures of their work and get their permission to share! The return on this investment of time will be monumental!

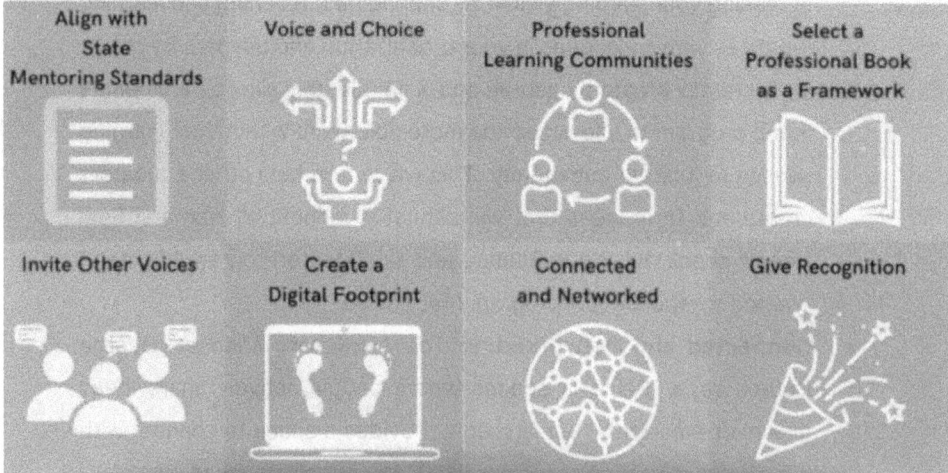

CHAPTER SEVEN

# Mentors Are All Around Us

## BY LAUREN M. KAUFMAN

*When we work together to help students succeed, the sky is the limit. We need each other to succeed so we can succeed ourselves.*

—ALLYSON APSEY

An educational ecosystem is made up of dedicated individuals who work tirelessly to nurture the social, emotional, and intellectual growth of kids. Each stakeholder, whether a group or individual, contributes unique perspectives that aid in the growth and evolution of the organizations in which they serve. As I move forward as an administrator in a formal leadership role, I am continually learning to navigate my surroundings with more intention and purpose. I view every person I encounter as a potential mentor and guide who can shape my vision and help me act with intent. The constantly changing landscape of education can sometimes feel new and unfamiliar, whatever stage of your career you're in. But, with the help of mentors, you can overcome any feelings of self-doubt that arise. With a collaborative spirit, collectively, you can continue to grow and learn within these evolving ecosystems.

## Embracing the Unfamiliar: Overcoming Fear and Finding Connection in New Environments

You have felt the kind of newness I'm talking about. You have stepped into new spaces and created your own narratives about them, leaving you feeling weary, judged, nervous, and perhaps confused. Just know that you don't have to embark on this journey alone. To navigate the diverse personalities and perspectives of an educational system, it is important to seek out mentors and support systems who can help ground your emotions and ignite your passion. That feeling of newness can take you back in time and unlock memories of the leader you didn't realize you were becoming. For example, when I was in middle school, I had to make a change in my academic schedule. This meant that I would have to endure a new lunch period, meet new people, and worry about where I would sit during one of the most awkward stages in my life. I'd have to find a seat with people who had already been sitting together for months. I created this story in my head that no one would want to sit with me. I thought about the possibility of standing in front of the lunchroom desperately searching for familiarity and acceptance.

And then, the actual day came. When I walked into the cafeteria, my eyes intensely and quickly scanned the room for a familiar face, a smile, eye contact—anything. Suddenly, I heard an unfamiliar voice say, "Hey, come over here and sit with us! So, do you remember holding the door open for me when I was walking into school earlier? I don't know how I would have made it inside alone because I was holding that big instrument case, my lunch bag, and a pile of books!" I finally exhaled and smiled back. "Oh yes, I did hold that door for you, didn't I? I was happy to help!"

The truth is, I didn't really remember holding the door. Holding a door for someone who needed help is just something I would naturally do, but to the person I helped, it meant the world. This interaction reminded me that even small acts of leadership and kindness can make a big difference in someone's day. This small significant moment in time also helped me break out of the negative narrative I created in my head, so I could courageously step into newness. As leaders, it is important to know that small actions can have a big impact on others. Putting others' needs before our own can cultivate a spirit of leadership that inspires those around us to do the same.

When you step into a new school or a new role, it can feel like the crowded lunchroom of unfamiliar faces. You don't know all of the people and you don't know if you will be welcomed. You don't know everyone's stories, their educational philosophies, or personal/professional goals. You can't always see how the small leadership moves embedded throughout busy days can become an investment in someone's emotional deposit box. That overwhelming feeling of newness can become frustrating, if you let it. But you were hired for a reason. You made it to this moment of newness because you have proven that you deserve to be here.

I'd like to think of myself as a proactive person who takes action swiftly, but when things are new, I find myself holding back a little more, listening more attentively, consuming all different types of information, trying to be more responsive and less reactive, and asking lots of questions. This was a shift in mindset when I stepped into the newness of leadership. I came to a place where I recognized that there is strength in pushing my pride to the side, asking questions, and leaning into the mentors all around me.

In the captivating book *Personal and Authentic: Designing Learning Experiences that Impact a Lifetime* by Thomas C. Murray, he bravely opens up about the power of vulnerability. From the very beginning, Murray shares a heartfelt story of the profound influence his mentor had on shaping his vision as an educator, and the lasting legacy he wished to leave for his students and colleagues. It was through this mentorship that Murray discovered the significance of creating meaningful moments rooted in strong relationships, empathy, and genuine care for children. His mentor's unwavering support guided him through the challenges of the teaching journey, instilling the virtue of patience and the importance of embracing the entire experience.[31]

This special bond between mentor and mentee profoundly impacted Murray's growth as an educator and helped him carve a path to success. Inspired by his mentor, Murray has gone on to unlock the untapped potential in others, captivating educators worldwide with his dynamic and influential stories that resonate deeply in their hearts and minds, leaving an everlasting impact.

Through his personal narrative, Murray reminds us that the key to making a difference lies in genuine connections and a commitment to nurturing the potential within each individual. His inspiring journey serves as a testament to the transformative power of mentorship and the profound influence it can have on shaping lives and educational experiences.

### The Spark that Ignites a Fire

The captivating stories in Murray's book *Personal and Authentic* sparked a profound introspection within me, evoking reflection about my relationship with my mentor during my early days as a teacher at P.S. 65 in Ozone Park, Queens. My mentor played a vital role in helping me navigate newness, guiding me toward a new reality, and igniting the spark that fueled my relentless educator spirit. While every detail of our significant moments together may have faded with time, her impact on me is an everlasting source of inspiration.

Drawing upon these cherished memories, I embarked on the task of pairing mentors and mentees as the mentor coordinator in my former school district. Understanding the profound importance of these relationships built on trust, hope, and promise, I could use my experiences to provide opportunities for the next generation of teachers and leaders to flourish.

The framework for what defines a mentor and leader was expertly exemplified by my first formal mentor, Mrs. Barbara Rubin, a seasoned teacher leader and former colleague. Seeking to honor our shared journey, I reached out to Barbara, hoping to weave her story into a blog post I wrote, "Unlocking Significant Moments in Time."[32] Little did Barbara know that her actions laid a solid foundation, serving as a beacon of guidance for future mentors and leaders. Together, we shared the stories that encapsulate our time as mentor and mentee, a testament to the transformative power of collaboration and growth. Below, I've included our written exchange from that post, which highlights the profound impact of a seemingly ordinary interaction, now memorialized in this book to serve as a source of inspiration for all.

When I was a first-year teacher, Barbara gave me the confidence I craved as I journeyed through my first-year teaching successes, challenges, and failures. Some of the qualities that Barbara possessed were her genuine kindness, patience, and content knowledge. She was extremely approachable and gave me the confidence and advice I needed to navigate relationships, protocols, and teaching and learning practices. One day, I vividly remember standing in front of the overhead projector (remember those?) "ready" to teach a writing lesson. After all, I had it written in my planbook, the learning objective was clearly written on a sentence strip, and was posted on the chalkboard, "Students will be able to write a good beginning of their story by hooking the reader." I looked around the room, stated the learning objective (that's what we called it at the time), and then . . . I completely froze. My inner voice said, "I know how to write, but how do I TEACH writing?" I pretended to look completely cool; I turned off the overhead projector and called Barbara. I whispered into the phone, "Barbara, how do you teach writing?" She laughed and responded in the most supportive way possible, "I'll be right there, don't worry!"

— LAUREN

As I began working with Lauren I soon realized that she was a natural for the teaching profession. She was not only bright, but compassionate, organized, willing to learn, and accepting of advice, as well as, (I hope) constructive criticism. I loved the way she spoke with her students, making each one feel special. You could see them glow after a conversation, even if she was correcting a behavior. Lauren also developed a great rapport with her colleagues. She was my first mentee after many, many years in the classroom. As the relationship grew, we both benefited. I imparted to Lauren what I had learned throughout my career and Lauren brought to me a fresh perspective and enthusiasm. I suppose you could say this is collaboration at its best. This is what the mentor/mentee program is all about.

— BARBARA

During my time with Barbara, I asked her questions, but probably not as many as I should have. Still, that relationship opened doors to me asking a multitude of questions to people I perceived as mentors in my various roles. Since becoming an administrator, I have been reflecting on the number of questions I ask the mentors around me. In fact, I'm certain I have asked far more questions stepping into the newness of a leadership role than I did when I was a teacher. You may find this funny, but when I catch myself reflecting on this idea, I actually ask myself, *Why so many questions, Lauren?* Leading can be hard. Leading can be fun. Leading can be draining, BUT teaching and leading is also the most incredibly rewarding career on the planet. With the right people in your corner, you can have a long, meaningful career. Knowing all these things, why didn't I seek them out to ask all the questions I know I needed answers to years ago? Perhaps I had not stepped into a courageous place in my journey. Maybe I wasn't in the mental space to understand that failure could be an asset, an opportunity to learn or try something new. Perhaps I didn't have the patience to refine my practices, iterate, fail, and improve. Perhaps I didn't realize that although setbacks can be discouraging, they are only temporary. Maybe I didn't know that as long as I was doing my best, I could be proud of my choices.

Recently, I had a check-in with a new teacher, similar to the way Barbara checked in on me. When I walked into her classroom, I could feel the newness of her learning ecosystem surrounding me. As I waited for her to finish up her conversations with students, I walked around and scanned the landscape of the room. I felt the learning emanating through her classroom walls, the energy of her kindness and enthusiasm for learning permeating into my heart. At the same time, I noticed that she had pulled up a seat next to a student who was feeling defeated. "What is making you feel this way? What can I do to help?" This new teacher was asking a student questions to build connection and get him to a more comfortable place.

When she was finished, I invited her to sit next to me at a small round table. I started to ask her some open-ended questions: "What's going well? What barriers may be getting in the way of your growth?" She led with this answer: "Lauren, I just need to say that I love it here. I really love it, Lauren. When I have questions, I know I can go to my colleagues for support." This answer made my face light up and smile so big that my cheeks started hurting. This new teacher had surpassed where I was at the beginning of my career and right then, I recognized the leader that was living inside her.

While speaking with her, I was instantaneously brought back to the new teacher interactions I had with a strong female leader, my first formal mentor, Barbara. In that moment, I knew she was rowing toward success and that I needed to be another strong female leader by continuing to elevate her gifts, harnessing her own leadership qualities, while encouraging her to reflect on the educator she is and who she wants to be. I went on to ask, "Now, what questions do you have for me?"

All the moments in your days are opportunities to seek out mentors and shape the educator you are continuously striving to be. Consider every interaction as a gift waiting to be unwrapped. Use those moments to uplift yourself and others, and you will never feel like you are in this work alone. The new teacher I mentioned above recently obtained a teaching role in another school district, and shared the following message with me after I asked her how things were going:

> Loving it! Still will never have the words to thank you enough for everything. You truly were a HUGE part in my growth as a teacher last year, and now a huge part of why I feel ready to have this brand new classroom of kiddos 🖤

I'll never forget a sentiment Ms. Leigh Dowden, a well-respected veteran teacher leader and community member, shared with me during my entry plan interview as a first-year administrator. As I expressed some nervousness stepping into a building leadership role, she said, "Lauren, in this work, there will always be a lot of balls in the air, and if one drops, you can count on one of us to catch it." Right then, I knew I had found another strong female mentor who would always be in my corner.

When I stepped into the newness of leadership, I stopped thinking about the way things are supposed to be. I stopped trying to work toward a place of perfection. The pathway to the outcomes you are searching for is not always linear. Sometimes, seeking advice from mentors, asking questions, and standing still in newness is the best way to move forward. Finding the courage to ask questions may be the action needed to harness momentum toward the leader you are becoming and the place you want to be.

## Actionable Ideas to Implement Tomorrow

A culture of mentorship begins with leaders who value its importance. When onboarding new teachers and nurturing aspiring leaders, consider implementing these ideas and questions for discussion to foster a mentorship culture within your leadership team. By prioritizing mentorship, leaders can cultivate supportive learning environments where everyone is invested in each other's success. In turn, nurturing a culture of mentorship can have a ripple effect throughout the learning ecosystem, ensuring greater collaboration and career well-being, and elevating student achievement.

- **Support New Teachers in Their Learning Ecosystem:** What strategies can leaders use to support and elevate new teachers in their learning ecosystems?
- **Encourage Educators to Seek Advice to Enhance Leadership Qualities:** How can leaders encourage their staff to ask questions and seek advice from mentors to enhance their leadership qualities?
- **Promote a Culture of Kindness, Enthusiasm, and Connection:** How can leaders promote a culture of kindness, enthusiasm, and connection in their learning environments?
- **Harness Your Own Leadership Qualities to Support the Growth of Colleagues:** How can leaders harness their own leadership qualities to elevate and support the growth of their colleagues and staff?

CHAPTER EIGHT

# Mirrors Shape Leaders

## BY LAUREN M. KAUFMAN

*May our feet be firmly planted in the soil of what is good: taking great care of people and their hope. And taking great care of ourselves and our hope, too.*

—MEGHAN LAWSON

### Nurturing Leaders: Embracing the Next Generation

In the realm of education, you've likely observed the vast potential for shaping the mindsets, actions, and choices of future generations throughout their educational journeys. Your role affords you unique opportunities to forge genuine connections and empower learners to take on new perspectives, leading to purposeful and joyful paths of success.

Allow me to share a heartwarming encounter that remains etched in my memory. In the first week of school, I stepped into a vibrant fifth-grade classroom and was warmly greeted by an enthusiastic teacher. I introduced myself: "Hello, everyone! I'm Mrs. Kaufman, the director of literacy here, essentially the district's reading and writing detective." Following my introduction, my eyes met those of a new student, Katherine, who chimed in, "Hello, Mrs. Kaufman.

I'm Katherine, and I'm new here!" I replied, "Welcome, Katherine! We're thrilled to have you here," and with curiosity, I asked, "Which school did you transfer from?" She answered, "I came from a school in Queens." Realizing there are nearly two thousand schools within the New York City Department of Education, I couldn't resist adding, "Well, Katherine, we already have something in common. Many years ago, I was a second-grade classroom teacher in that very same school." Her smile illuminated the room, and together, we celebrated the moment with a selfie. It serves as a beautiful reminder that life has a way of guiding us precisely where we are meant to be.

This heartwarming encounter from my own journey exemplifies the profound impact educators can have, and it seamlessly transitions into the critical role you play in supporting your colleagues and the future leaders you help nurture.

Given the ever-evolving nature of education, it is crucial that educators like you are equipped with essential tools and robust support systems to navigate the dynamic landscape, uplift others, tackle challenges, and adapt to change. These supports can empower your colleagues to cultivate agency, self-efficacy, and the confidence to share their unique strengths, ultimately unlocking the potential of every individual they encounter on their educational journeys. You also understand the value of time and the delicate balance managing it requires. Every minute, every interaction, every moment in your day holds tremendous value, like the interaction mentioned above. Among the myriad ways to invest your time, mentorship stands out for its exceptional return on investment, as you play a pivotal role in shaping the next generation of leaders.

There is no magic wand for mentoring. The success of strong mentor/mentee relationships rests on the shoulders of WHO. WHO puts in the effort, WHO has the sensibility, WHO has the dedication, and WHO commits to the process. All of these things matter, but a little bit of strategy goes along with this, too. I mention *strategy* because it is vital to consider WHO will be the right people to guide and create strong foundations for new teachers and leaders that will lead to long, meaningful, impactful careers. In an episode of Brené Brown's *Dare to Lead* podcast, "Brené with Jim Collins on Curiosity, Generosity, and the Hedgehog," Jim Collins discusses the importance of inviting people into your life who will open the doors to greatness. "Pick great people in your life. Those people are your mirror and will tell you if you're doing OK."[33] The idea of viewing the people in your life as a mirror of yourself only magnifies the significance of WHO is placed in a position to mentor, inspire, and influence teachers during the new teacher induction process.

In previous chapters, I delved into the profound connections I fostered with individuals I regarded as mentors. These remarkable individuals possessed the exceptional ability to recognize the leader living inside me. Moreover, I recounted some of the invaluable lessons gleaned from encounters with individuals who, for various reasons, may have refrained from fully harnessing my leadership potential. I am genuinely appreciative of these experiences as well, for they played a crucial role in propelling me forward, enabling me to wholeheartedly embrace the successes and challenges that awaited me, unveiling new opportunities. Undoubtedly, they have all played an instrumental role in shaping the leader I am becoming.

Before I embark on telling another story, it is crucial to establish a clear understanding of the profound roles a mentor and mentee play. Let us delve into the essence of this symbiotic relationship and allow its significance to remain at the forefront of your mind as you navigate the evolving landscape of your educational journey.

## A mentor/mentee is someone WHO:

| A Mentor is someone WHO: | A Mentee is someone WHO: |
|---|---|
| ◄ | SYMBIOTIC ► |
| • Serves as a model for professionalism & trust | • Commits to the mentoring process |
| • Possesses a desire to develop long-term relationships & grow future leaders | • Places an emphasis on developing relationships |
| • Innately wants to see others succeed | • Focuses on continuously maximizing their personal & professional growth |
| • Commits time & energy to the Mentor/Mentee relationship | • Creates meaningful & relevant professional goals |
| • Imparts their knowledge & expertise openly & willingly | • Communicates strengths & areas for growth |
| • Stays current in best teaching & learning practices | • Asks for help, shows vulnerability, & is willing to explore different pathways & perspectives |
| • Shares successes, failures, & personal experiences | • Collaborates with PLCs, expands their PLN, & tries new practices |
| • Invites mentees into professional learning communities (PLCs) & encourages them to expand their professional learning networks (PLNs) | • Seeks & accepts constructive feedback |
| | • Holds themselves responsible & accountable |
| • Maintains an infinite mindset to learning & growth | • Maintains an infinite mindset to learning & growth |

**LAURENMKAUFMAN.COM | @LAURENMKAUFMAN**

Whenever an educator reaches out to me, I prioritize connecting with them, offering a listening ear and a beacon of hope. During one such conversation, an aspiring female administrator confided in me, saying, "Lauren, I'm unsure if I'm truly cut out for leadership. Despite my efforts, I always seem to fall just short of reaching the finish line. I think it might be time for me to take a break from applying."

This remark brought back memories of my own handful of interview experiences and the moments when I questioned if leadership was truly my path. The weight of disappointment pressed upon me, but I can still hear Linda Roth's voice, reminding me that this is all part of the process. I responded to this aspiring leader by saying, "No, you have to keep going. There is a district who will see that you are the person who is meant to be on their bus. This fleeting moment of rejection and doubt is an opportunity for a new door to open. So, remember that this setback is temporary. It's a marker on your journey. Keep pushing forward; the right opportunity with the right people is waiting for you."

In his book *Good to Great*, Collins discusses how hiring people who are aligned with your vision and direction will lead to avenues of great realizations, progress, and prosperity. Getting the "right people" on the bus because of "who" is on it rather than being concerned about "where" it is going makes it easier to change your course. "For no matter what we achieve, if we don't spend the vast majority of our time with people we love and respect, we cannot possibly have a great life. But if we spend the vast majority of our time with people we love and respect—people we really enjoy being on the bus with and who will never disappoint us—then we will almost certainly have a great life, no matter where the bus goes."[34]

Over the course of my professional journey, I've witnessed great educators doing exceptional things amid the changes the educational landscape presents. The finest educators and leaders I have ever known harness the energy and gifts of the people around them to bring their expertise to a team. They view every person on the bus as a puzzle piece that contributes to a bigger picture.

## A Shift in Perspective

As my career has progressed, I've found myself less impressed by educators' ability to deliver flashy presentations or their depth of knowledge in their field. Instead, I've become deeply intrigued by their capacity to include others in crucial discussions prior to making decisions, their active commitment to listening to the needs of their learning communities, and their dedication to ensuring everyone has a seat at the table. They embrace a variety of perspectives, ensuring the ideas can continue to propel a school district's mission, vision, and priorities forward. We have all experienced moments where our voices felt ignored, leaving us disheartened rather than empowered. As educational leaders, I know that we will not always be perfect, but it is crucial to ask ourselves whether we are creating spaces that illuminate the gifts and contributions others bring to the table—or simply highlighting our own.

I vividly recall the echoes of something Stephanie Rothstein (an innovator and my friend, as well as a contributor to this book) said resonating in my mind: "Education should be less competitive and more collaborative." Her profound sentiment also brings to mind Shawn Achor's insightful book, *Big Potential: How Transforming the Pursuit of Success Raises Our Achievement, Happiness, and Well-Being*, where he imparts a valuable message: "Success isn't solely determined by how creative, smart, or driven you are, but by your ability to connect with, contribute to, and benefit from the ecosystem of people around you."[35] With this in mind, I pose the question: How can leaders nurture educational communities that harness the collective growth and empowerment of the educators within them?

Achor's wisdom continues to inspire with his notion that "We spend the first twenty-two years of our life being judged and praised for our individual attributes and what we can achieve alone, when for the rest of our life, our success is almost entirely interconnected with that of others."[36] This concept deeply resonates with me, especially this year, as I face a number of literacy priorities to continue moving forward. I recognize the importance of not embarking on this journey solo. It was during my time as an instructional coach that I fully grasped the significance of building capacity from within your educational organization. After all, those educators working tirelessly on the front lines possess invaluable insights and a profound understanding of the needs at hand.

## Moving Forward

Recently, I received a call from that aspiring female leader mentioned above. "Lauren, you were right. After our conversation, I picked my head up and held it high. I learned from those disappointments, and now an amazing district wants me on their bus. I did it. Thank you."

By nurturing and mentoring the leaders around you and embracing the next generation, you can navigate changes, challenges, and systems to provide the best support for your colleagues. It will always be crucial to choose the right people on your path to guide you on your leadership journey. Keep surrounding yourself with people who act as mirrors, encourage you to reflect on your growth, and show you that there are other possibilities and more open doors leading to the right opportunities.

## Actionable Ideas to Implement Tomorrow

### The 6 Cs to Successful Mentor/Mentee Relationships

The mentor/mentee relationship is symbiotic in nature. The qualities and attributes in both mentees and mentors are synonymous. As you seek mentors and embrace mentorship, approach it from a holistic lens. You have the power to build social capital and unlock human potential. Great leaders have the ability to leave everlasting legacies in the hearts and minds of everyone they serve. This makes the induction years a critical component of a leader's career path. That's why I created a blueprint to sustain successful mentor/mentee relationships by embracing the 6 Cs: *Connect. Communicate. Collaborate. Circulate. Cultivate. Celebrate.*

- **Connect:** Get to know each other on a personal level. Share your stories. This will transform the path of a mentoring relationship because you are showing the other person that you care about them as a human first. This is a window into a person's journey that enables you to make more intentional and targeted inquiries over time. As Jim Collins says in the *Dare to Lead* podcast, "Real conversations happen at the feeling level . . . The quality of the day is not what you think about it, it's what you feel about it."[37]
- **Communicate:** Although informal interactions will naturally be embedded into the mentoring experience, schedule protected time to communicate on personal and professional levels. This protected time values the process and provides a space to ask questions, share knowledge, and learn from various experiences. Come up with mutually agreeable ways to communicate as there are many avenues to reach out to one another. Talking through and reflecting on experiences are important parts of the growth process.
- **Collaborate:** Work together to strengthen and share best teaching and learning practices, and how to navigate relationships and day-to-day operations. Collaboration can transpire synchronously by interacting face-to-face, in online meetings, texting, and/or instant messaging through various learning management systems. It can also take place asynchronously by working independently and then uploading documents or annotations to shared workspaces (e.g., Google Docs). The benefits of mentor/mentee collaboration are exploring new and better ideas and teamwork as well as discovering new solutions and embedding new perspectives into practices.
- **Circulate:** Mentors can be well-connected since they have been in the education field for some time. They should invite their mentees into various professional learning communities (PLCs) and encourage them to look for ideas beyond their own school organizations by expanding their professional learning network (PLN). As a mentor, you can also broaden your own network by connecting with other

mentors and great educators, while leveraging the opportunity to network with your mentee's connections.

- **Cultivate:** Mentees come with their own expertise and gifts to share. Help them unwrap those gifts, passions, and interests. Capitalize on, cultivate, and learn from their strengths. Ask questions and allow them to reflect on their areas for growth and development. Use this as an opportunity to let them come up with actionable steps for improvement while providing direction and insight. These interactions are cyclical in nature and should be continuously revisited.
- **Celebrate:** Mentors serve as the greatest and most impactful support system. They should encourage and cheer on their mentees for taking risks and believing in themselves. Celebrate successes big and small, and use failure and change as opportunities for growth. Human beings thrive on recognition. When we feel validated and valued, we continue to approach our work with passion and purpose!

# PART III:

# Stories of Impact and Courage

CHAPTER NINE

# The Leader Inside

## BY LAUREN M. KAUFMAN

> We need to accept that we won't always make the right decisions, that we'll screw up royally sometimes—understanding that failure is not the opposite of success, it's part of success.
>
> —ARIANNA HUFFINGTON

*L*eadership rests on the shoulders of influence and inspiration, not compliance and control. Leadership is not a title, but an opportunity to recognize the greatness that lives inside others. It's not about taking the credit for the work, but giving it to others. Leadership is about inspiring others to cultivate confidence in themselves so they can breathe life into ideas that will awaken their soul. Leadership is harnessing the gifts that are manifesting within. It's letting others recognize their potential by planting seeds they can nurture and grow. It's coming to peace with the idea of living publicly in your imperfection. Meghan Lawson once shared in an X post, "We don't find ourselves, we build ourselves. With every experience, setback, and bounce back, we learn and we build ourselves. And that's an energizing way to live in our own stories. Let's keep doing the work. Let's keep building."

## Salute the Person

Growing up, I had leaders all around me. My dad was one of them. He is a well-respected educator who puts people first. In fact, since he was an educator in the town where I grew up, we could not stop at a local restaurant or store without his former students running up to him and thanking him for his kindness and support, and the lessons learned from his classes. I still live there, and the first thing people ask me is, "How is your dad, Lauren? Please send him my best; he had a positive impact on me." Although my dad didn't hold a formal leadership title, I always knew he was a leader who left a legacy of influence in the hearts and minds of his students and colleagues. He learned this from his father, who was a leader in his community and spent a lot of his time giving back to people who were less fortunate than he was. As I have journeyed through my childhood, teen, and adult years, I've turned to my dad for advice. One of the pieces of advice he continues to share is, "Lauren, leaders salute the person, not the title. There is a leader inside us all."

I have navigated close to two decades in education, and those words still live in my mind. I am a natural observer of people. I take great interest in what others say, do, and act on. I look closely at the body language, reactions, and responses of others. I try to understand others' perspectives and have empathy for the hidden stories I cannot see. When reflecting on the people I have saluted throughout my life in any capacity, the common gift they possess is the ability to lead through inspiration. I can still hear and see the leaders who didn't limit my potential; instead, they fueled it. Now that I have formally stepped into leadership, I often reflect on the experiences that shaped the leader I am becoming.

Here are some ideas and stories that have inspired me to unleash the leader inside. See if you can connect them to stories in your own life.

**Trusting People:** My fifth-grade teacher saw the leader inside of me. She recognized a shy girl's potential to lead and support others. She chose *me* to take on the responsibility of being a first-grade class helper. Every Friday morning, I woke up with some extra pep in my step. I knew that I would be spending a period in Ms. Miller's first-grade classroom, where she gave me the responsibility of facilitating a small reading group. It felt so good to feel important, to sit in front of a group of students and model what it meant to be a good reader, even though I was a reader who had challenges of my own. Looking back, I think my fifth-grade teacher knew I lacked confidence with reading and asked a first-grade teacher to let me lead this work so I could develop confidence. In his book *Trust and Inspire*, Stephen Covey shares, "Operating with a trust and inspire mindset means you manage things and you lead people."[38] When we lead people by elevating them, it helps them to recognize their strengths. They may not see the power of that move in the moment, but they will eventually recognize its impact.

**Asking Good Questions:** My superintendent shared the article "A Beautiful Question" by Jim Knight with our leadership team during a professional learning session. Knight shares, "Good questions are real manifestations of your curiosity and caring. Good questions are like intellectual fireworks, leading to explosions of ideas and more learning for the questioner and the conversation partner."[39] Although I highly recommend this article, there are two ideas I want to highlight. One is that my superintendent is masterful at planting seed ideas within the people she serves. She is always sharing resources, quotes, and thoughts that spark collaboration and innovation among her team. I have seen this happen through a simple group text message. All she has to do is share an article in a text and ask one question: "What do you think?" This brings me to my second idea: great questions can lead to more creative and meaningful conversations. Once the article is in the group text, it takes minutes before there is an explosion of conversation in the thread between her leadership team. I have seen new ideas implemented only days after the intellectual fireworks commenced! She is leveraging our intellectual power and elevating the leaders inside us.

**Choosing Words Wisely:** When bringing out the leader in people, we must recognize the powerful impact words have on ourselves and others. In the book *The Four Agreements: A Practical Guide to Personal Freedom* by Don Miguel Ruiz, there is a chapter titled "Be Impeccable With Your Words." I curated these quotes from that chapter:

- "Your word is the power that you have to create."
- "The word is a force; it is the power you have to express and communicate, to think, and thereby to create the events in your life."
- "Through the word you express your creative power. It is through the word that you manifest everything."
- "The human mind is like a fertile ground where seeds are continuously being planted."
- "Being impeccable with your word is the correct use of your energy; it means to use your energy in the direction of truth and love for yourself."[40]

Everyone's perception is their reality. As leaders, when we are mindful of the words we use, we can better help others recognize the leader that lives inside them. You can help others shape their perception of themselves by positively communicating ideas, intention, and purpose. This helps instill happiness, bringing out the best in those you serve. Those actions directly impact every stakeholder in your organization including those at the heart of it all, the students.

## Leading Together

Leading and learning together is a privilege. Opportunities to grow ideas and collaborate with others in your educational organization are all around you. The energy you exude as a leader can significantly impact the people you lead. If you acknowledge what you can't accomplish given the vast scope of your work, others will be willing to step in, support you, and make meaningful contributions to the mission and vision of the organization. True growth transcends individual limitations when you leverage the collective experiences and expertise of the people around you. When you limit your work to your own perspective, it's an invitation to build unnecessary barriers and miss out on invaluable insights that can propel your team to success. In the book *Lead Like a Teacher: How to Elevate Expertise in Your School* by Miriam Plotinsky, she shares, "It became increasingly clear that when leaders and teachers work together consistently with a shared desire to help students achieve, they are close to unstoppable."[41]

As a leader dedicated to learning with and from others, you intend to navigate your days with authenticity and an open heart and mind. In trying to connect with others and value the purpose of the work, you can see people and things in ways you may not have noticed before. Unearthing new ideas in unexpected places opens doors to fresh possibilities, even in the face of obstacles that can impede the optimal level of student success.

When I was a teacher, I attended a local conference with other teacher leaders and a large group of administrators. In the morning, we attended various sessions where we expressed how excited we were to learn new things to bring back to our school district. I'll never forget the next part of this story. During lunch, my colleagues and I sat with a few administrators, while a larger group of administrators sat at another table. Suddenly, the administrators who had joined our table abruptly left to join their colleagues. It felt awkward because their table was overcrowded, while ours had empty seats. To me, this action created a noticeable divide between teachers and administrators. *Would it have been more beneficial to allow quality time and inclusive conversations with educators who work directly with students and teachers to help move our schools forward?* This missed opportunity highlights how leaders can be more intentional in creating opportunities for educators to come together. Sharing, thinking, and learning can bridge the gap between the role of an administrator and teacher, helping others discover the leader that lives inside them.

If you have been entrusted to work with kids, someone has faith in your ability to model the behaviors you want to instill in the students and colleagues around you. Therefore, the relationship between leaders, colleagues, and staff must be symbiotic in nature. By leveling the playing field and leaving egos at the door, stakeholders can work together toward a common goal. Plotinsky also added this sentiment in her book: "When teachers and leaders do not seek to understand one another, that becomes one of the largest untapped barriers to school progress."[42] The time we take to reflect together and talk about ideas and share our successes and challenges can become pivotal moments that help leaders capitalize on the expertise of those around us. In his book *The Obstacle Is the Way*, Ryan Holiday shared, "Where one person sees a crisis, another can see opportunity."[43]

That said, *how can we build social capital by coming together to share meaningful ideas that can have a positive impact on the organizations we live in?*

## Actionable Ideas to Implement Tomorrow

- **Intentionally Embrace Shared Experiences:** Recently, I attended a local conference with a few of the teachers I lead. The experience I just shared about the conference I attended years ago has stayed with me. Even though I was meeting an old friend and colleague at this recent conference, I made sure to get there early and save seats for the teachers I work with. That morning, I found them on the other side of the room and immediately invited them to join me at the table. This small move ensured that we could connect and share ideas. In turn, they surprised me by attending the session I was facilitating, even though I tried to convince them to attend another! This strengthened our leader–teacher connection because I made the space for that time together.
- **Proximity Counts:** When I facilitate department meetings, it's always important to me to sit *with* teachers. I often position my chair so it

appears that I am not the only "leader" of the meeting. This sends the message that "your voice matters" and "you are an important contributor to this discussion." Sitting with teachers and being physically closer to them allows me to pay closer attention to cues such as body language, facial expressions, and tone of voice. This helps me better understand their perspectives, which builds trust, cultivates community, and strengthens future communication and collaboration.
- **Reflective Questioning Grows Ideas:** Recently I facilitated a secondary department meeting, where I asked these questions:
  - What were some of your most successful teaching moments this year, and why do you think they were successful?
  - What advice would you give to yourself at the beginning of the school year, based on what you know now?

After providing some wait time, these questions opened up a wide range of discussion and allowed teachers to share best practices in an authentic way. These learning spaces create an environment where ideas are valued and learning is prioritized. At the end of the meeting, a veteran teacher I greatly admire said, "What I just learned is that I need to talk to my colleagues more about what they are doing. I'd like to add more creativity to my teaching."

## Moving Forward

The leaders who inspired me to become a leader always considered their teachers more important than themselves. *How will you commit to creating spheres of influence that ensure teachers and leaders are leading and learning together?* I can assure you that being intentional with this time will be a critical investment in the social capital deposit box. Never miss an opportunity to lead together and discover the leadership qualities that live within others; these moments will propel your students and colleagues toward success. When you salute the person and not the title, there is greater potential to find more leaders living among us. You have the potential to rekindle and ignite the spirit and joy within others. Great leaders inspire others to have confidence inside themselves. People yearn to be inspired. Breathe life into their gifts and ideas and show them the leader that awaits inside.

With nearly twenty years of experience in education, **Natasha Nurse** is a dedicated professional known for her innovative work in teaching, learning, and community service. Currently, she serves as a middle school STEM teacher, where she has developed a unique curriculum focused on nurturing curiosity and helping students discover their passions.  Natasha also holds the role of mentor coordinator K–12, providing support to new teachers and collaborating on elevating student learning experiences by instituting a new mentor program for high school students. Her career has included roles as an elementary classroom teacher and instructional coach for grades K–5. Natasha appreciates sharing her learning with the greater educational community by presenting at national and local conferences. Outside of education, Natasha chairs the Long Beach Housing Authority, emphasizing community development. Her extensive experiences continue to inspire others in both education and community work. You can connect with Tasha on X (@Natasha_Nurse) and on Instagram (@tnurselb).

CHAPTER TEN

# Through the Glass Ceiling
## Breaking Barriers and Forging New Paths

**BY NATASHA NURSE**

*Every child deserves a champion—an adult who will never give up on them, who understands the power of connection, and insists that they become the best that they can possibly be.*

—RITA PIERSON

Can I honestly add on to a plate that is already filled with so many things? This question echoes in my mind, serving as a constant reminder of the responsibilities I carry as a wife, mother, and educator. Each day, I find myself reflecting on my journey, the road I have traveled, and the journey that lies ahead.

In this process, one truth stands out among the others: it is in the collective effort of many that we can truly make a difference in our communities.

### Family Legacy: A Father's Dedication

From a tender age, my passion for community was undeniable, largely influenced by my father's unwavering commitment to service. As a police officer, he exuded pride and dedication, often volunteering to address students in our schools. Through stories of grit, he kindled a spirit of resilience, teaching the importance of pushing through. His role as the first African American officer in the Long Beach, New York, Police Department was more than a personal milestone; it was a beacon for others, signifying change and hope.

I fondly recall evenings spent in our living room, my siblings and I intently listening to Dad recount tales from his younger years in the south. His narratives, detailed with challenges and triumphs, were rich with life's lessons. Among them, the essence of genuine relationships stood out. He believed that true connections rose above differences and backgrounds—a philosophy I deeply resonate with. Stories of his time at the Long Beach Police Department were particularly memorable, filled with tales of camaraderie and mutual respect. He always maintained, "Being trustworthy is the first step to gaining trust."

Beyond his duties as an officer, he also devoted time to our local Martin Luther King Center, serving as a board member. Here, he channeled his leadership into framing policies that backed the center's director and, in turn, enriched the lives of countless families. My father's bravery, especially during challenging times, remains a legacy not just for me but for our entire community, shaping the ethos of our beloved hometown.

## Pursuing a Purpose: Educator and Community Organizer

Teaching itself demands an immense amount of time and energy, but I envisioned more. I yearned for a future where I could utilize my love for the community where I work and live to raise awareness of the needs of the families living within it. In building relationships with my students, it wasn't enough to solely focus on teaching the curriculum; their stories, their truths, were equally important. George Couros beautifully highlights the importance of relationships in his book *The Innovator's Mindset*. He states, "If we want meaningful change, we have to make a connection to the heart before we can make a connection to the mind. Spending time developing relationships and building trust is crucial to moving forward as a whole. Without culture, there is no culture of innovation. It all starts by creating an environment where people feel cared for, supported, and nurtured—the very things we know that impact learning for students in the classroom."[44] Driven by determination, I focused on creating such an environment! However, I was also keenly aware of the unique challenges I faced as a female leader and person of color. The path I envisioned for myself as an educator and community organizer was not without obstacles. I knew that breaking through the glass ceiling and overcoming systemic barriers would require resilience and determination.

To equip myself with the knowledge and understanding needed to effect change, I sought to immerse myself in the intricacies of our school community and the broader community beyond. I joined various school committees and district committees, dedicating my time and effort to understanding the needs, concerns, and aspirations of the diverse stakeholders involved.

Engaging with a variety of stakeholders brought its own challenges. Complex interactions, each person with their unique perspective and concern, sometimes left me wondering what else could I possibly bring to the table. Amid this whirlwind, a fear lurked in the background—the fear of making a mistake. Serving in influential roles made me cautious, every decision analyzed and reanalyzed, always aiming to be the epitome of trustworthiness.

Navigating the committee meetings and engaging in discussions allowed me to gain valuable insights into our educational system, the challenges faced by students, teachers, and families, and the potential avenues for positive transformation. It wasn't always easy to balance these additional responsibilities alongside my role as an educator and my personal commitments. At times, the weight of responsibilities like crafting lesson plans, preparing for community board meetings, or addressing the concerns of dissatisfied community members felt overwhelming. Doubts occasionally surfaced, making me question the impact of my efforts. Yet, in those moments, I'd recall the profound influence my father had on me and the legacy he left behind. This spurred me on, reminding me that every action, regardless of its size, can propel progress and empowerment. I continued to voice my thoughts, share my insights, and suggest innovations, knowing that each effort was a step toward a more inclusive education for all.

## The Influence of a Mentor

Mrs. Sandy Schneider, my principal at the time, played an instrumental role in shaping my journey. Sandy epitomized a unique blend of being both firm and deeply compassionate. She consistently stood by families, guiding them through both celebrations and challenges. A piece of wisdom she frequently imparted was, "Always bridge the gap between home and school; that's where real impact is made." This belief in the profound importance of giving back and the crucial link between home and school has had a lasting influence on me. As fate would have it, we crossed paths again. Sandy is now my supervisor as I undertake my administrative internship in the very same school district where she hired me as a teacher and served as my principal.

I distinctly remember our heartfelt discussions where I eagerly shared my aspirations of making a positive impact on the community. It was during one of these conversations that the Martin Luther King Center emerged as a significant opportunity. Sandy's encouragement and insightful feedback fueled my passion and conviction. With her words echoing in my mind—"Go for it, Tasha! You have the potential to make a difference"—I felt compelled to take action.

As I sat in Sandy's office, the room filled with the subtle hum of distant conversations. I leaned forward, enthusiasm evident in my eyes. "I've always wanted to truly make a mark on our community, Sandy," I said.

She looked at me intently, her expression a mixture of curiosity and encouragement. "Have you considered the Martin Luther King Center?" she asked, her voice hinting at a promising avenue.

A moment of surprise crossed my face. "The MLK Center? I've thought about it, but—"

Sandy interrupted, her voice steady and full of conviction, "Tasha, I've seen your dedication and your heart." She leaned in, placing a reassuring hand on my shoulder. "Go for it. You've got this."

With eagerness, I embraced the opportunity to volunteer in the Martin Luther King's Center Homework Afterschool Program and dedicated my time and effort as a board member. These integral roles granted me the privilege to contribute to the center's mission and become part of the initiative to establish a deep connection between the school and the community. Through my involvement, I aimed to cultivate an environment characterized by trust, understanding, and collaboration where students, families, and educators could unite their strengths to generate positive change and foster holistic development. I had the privilege of witnessing firsthand the transformative power it held for the students who actively participated. The impact on their lives was undeniable, and it became clear to me that we needed to fortify and expand the program's reach to ensure that more students could benefit from this invaluable resource.

## Engaging Community and Empowering Families

With determination to effect change, I reached out to Dr. Anael Alston, who is currently the assistant commissioner of New York State Education but, at the time, served as the principal of Glen Cove Middle School and possessed a wealth of experience in community organizing. Recognizing his expertise, I extended an invitation to Dr. Alston to speak at our Second Annual Education Fair, which took place at the Martin Luther King Center.

Throughout the planning process for the event, I had support and guidance from Sandy. Her enthusiasm for the Education Fair was exciting, and she played a pivotal role in helping me bring the vision to life. With her knowledge and experience, she provided guidance on organizing the schedule, coordinating the various activities, and ensuring the event's seamless flow.

The Second Annual Education Fair held at the Martin Luther King Center received overwhelming support from district leaders, including our superintendent. Their recognition of the fair's significance in fostering meaningful connections between the school district and the wider community bolstered our confidence and reinforced the importance of our mission.

The day of the Education Fair, the Martin Luther King Center buzzed with excitement and anticipation. Dr. Alston delivered a captivating keynote address, highlighting the importance of bridging the gap between home and school to create an inclusive and supportive learning environment for students. His inspiring words resonated with the attendees and set the tone for the evening ahead. District leaders organized insightful breakout sessions specifically tailored for parents, which provided an opportunity for open discussions on topics such as effective communication, parental involvement, and strategies for supporting student learning. The intention behind these sessions was to empower parents with the knowledge and skills necessary to actively participate in their children's education and create a strong foundation for academic success.

As I reflect on the impact of the fair, I see that the event served as a testament to the power of community mobilization and the profound difference that can be made when individuals come together with a shared purpose. It underscored the notion that by embracing our roles as educators, leaders, and community members, we have the potential to create positive, lasting change in the lives of those we serve. Moments of clarity and connection emerged from this endeavor as well. I witnessed the blossoming trust between families and teachers. The impact of my efforts and others became evident in the smiles of students who felt supported and understood. I realized that community engagement was not an additional burden; it was an opportunity to bridge gaps and create a sense of unity. This connection with my students has helped me thrive in the classroom as I continue to build strong relationships by understanding the needs of all students.

Looking back on the impact my principal, Sandy Schneider, has had on my life, I am so thankful for her support and genuine belief in my ability to make a difference. Sandy's mentorship has been inspirational, shaping not only my path as an educator but also instilling in me a deep sense of purpose and a steadfast dedication to serving the needs of our school community. Her guidance has left a lasting imprint on my heart that continues to inspire and motivate me in my current pursuit of receiving my administration license.

Through my experiences, I have grown both personally and professionally. I have learned the power of kindness and gratitude. I have become a better educator, able to tailor my teaching approaches to meet the unique needs of each student. I have also become a stronger advocate for my community, standing up for the voices that may feel silenced. In Lainie Rowell's book *Evolving with Gratitude*, she highlights the connection between kindness and gratitude. She says, "The connection between kindness and gratitude in our world is significant and undeniable, but we don't always take the time to think about how the two are connected. Both are contagious and benefit all involved. You can find both in unexpected places, and together, kindness and gratitude can create a loop of positivity that makes us more resilient."[45] Showing kindness and gratitude has indeed helped me become more resilient and focused on bridging the home–school connection.

As a woman leader, I understand of the importance of representation and the pivotal role that a variety of perspectives play in positions of influence. Throughout my journey, I have encountered numerous challenges and obstacles that resonate deeply with many women in leadership roles. However, rather than being deterred by these experiences, they have fueled my determination to continue breaking down barriers and forging pathways for the next generation of women leaders eager to make a positive impact in their communities.

## Community Involvement Beyond Education

I am currently serving as the board chair of the Housing Authority in Long Beach, New York. I'm truly proud to be part of a team dedicated to creating positive change in our community. As a woman leader, I bring a unique perspective and approach to the table, one that prioritizes empathy, collaboration, and collective decision-making. I firmly believe that varied voices and experiences lead to more comprehensive and effective solutions. I have also witnessed the transformative power of stable and affordable housing, particularly for women and their families. Housing stability not only provides a sense of security and dignity, but it also empowers individuals to thrive and pursue their goals. I've seen firsthand how stable housing serves as a foundation for success in other areas of life, such as education, employment, and overall well-being.

I am inspired by the trailblazing women who have come before me, those who have shattered glass ceilings and paved the way for progress. Their resilience and bravery serves as a constant reminder that we have the power to effect change, even in the face of adversity.

As I look ahead, I am reminded of the challenges and rewards that come with stepping outside of our comfort zones. While my plate may be full at times, within it lies endless possibilities. Each day, I strive to take small steps, to make a lasting impact on the lives of those I serve. And with each small step, I encourage others who may feel overwhelmed by their own plates to find a way to contribute, volunteer, bridge the gap, and build trust between families and educators. For it is in the collective effort of many that we can truly make a difference in our communities. As educators, we have the incredible opportunity to make a meaningful impact on our students' lives and the communities we serve. The following ideas have helped me in my journey of community work.

## Actionable Ideas to Implement Tomorrow

- **Volunteer at a Local Community Center:** Dedicate some of your time to help students with their homework or participate in after-school programs.
- **Join or Create School Committees:** Get involved in committees that focus on addressing the needs of the community.
- **Establish Partnerships with Local Organizations:** Reach out to local organizations, such as nonprofits or businesses, that align with your school's mission and values.
- **Organize Community Events:** Plan and organize events that bring together families, educators, and community members.
- **Develop Service-Learning Projects:** Integrate service-learning into your curriculum by designing projects that allow students to address real community needs.
- **Engage in Professional Learning:** Seek out professional learning opportunities that focus on community engagement.
- **Amplify Student Voice:** Create platforms for students to share their perspectives and ideas on how to improve the school and community.

## Collaboration and Resilience

I have learned that no one person can do it all alone. It takes a collective effort, a symphony of voices and perspectives, to truly effect change. In the continuation of my journey, I will keep seeking out opportunities for collaboration, knowing that together we can make a difference.

I am grateful for the support and encouragement I have received thus far. The commitment of my father, the mentorship of influential educators such as my principal, Sandy Schneider, and the guidance of community leaders have all played a pivotal role in shaping my path. Their belief in me and their shared vision of making a positive difference have inspired me to embrace my role as an educator wholeheartedly. In their guidance, I have found not only inspiration but also a sense of camaraderie among like-minded individuals who are passionate about creating change.

Simultaneously, I am filled with hope for the future. I recognize the power of education and the profound impact it can have on individuals and communities. Therefore, I extend an invitation to women from all walks of life to embark on their own journeys of purpose and reflection. Take a moment to reflect on the responsibilities you carry, the communities you serve, and the immense power of collaboration. Embrace the idea of adding to your plate, taking on new challenges, and inviting others to join you in this life-changing journey. Together, let us weave a tapestry of impact that inspires change, fosters growth, and instills a sense of purpose in the lives of those we touch.

**Linda Roth** is an educator whose passion is inspiring students and fostering educational excellence. With a career spanning four decades, Linda has assumed the roles of special education teacher, general education teacher, assistant principal, director of curriculum and technology, and assistant superintendent for curriculum and instruction. Graduating with honors from Hofstra University, she earned a bachelor's degree in education and a master's degree in special education. Driven by a commitment to lifelong learning, she later earned a certificate of advanced studies in educational administration and leadership. In her role of teacher, her goal was to foster an environment where each student could reach their highest potential and embrace a lifelong love for learning. In her role of administrator, she fostered a supportive workplace culture for staff, where collaboration, professional development, and mutual respect flourished. Beyond her official roles and professional achievements, Linda is a mentor and shares her wisdom and experiences to empower the next generation of educators and leaders. Through her work, she has left an enduring impact on students, colleagues, and the educational community at large.

## CHAPTER ELEVEN

# Eternal Memories Manifest Hope for the Future

### BY LAUREN M. KAUFMAN AND LINDA ROTH

> *If you're going to live, leave a legacy. Make a mark on the world that can't be erased.*
>
> —MAYA ANGELOU

Enduring connections and relationships have a profound impact on everyone—teachers, students, and mentors alike. Even the memory of these connections can provide eternal hope and inspiration on your educational and professional path.

### My Eternal Mental Movie

In the introduction to this book, I mentioned my beloved fourth-grade teacher, Mrs. Roth. It's astounding how that single moment when I entered her classroom set in motion a lifelong connection that continues to shape my educational journey to this very day. Mrs. Roth was the extraordinary individual who saw the seeds of leadership within me, even as a young girl, and wholeheartedly believed in my potential, even during those times when my confidence wavered and my reading abilities posed challenges. Our bond has remained unyielding throughout the years. From those early grade-school days to her invaluable guidance while preparing me for my first administrative interviews, and her ongoing mentorship as I navigate the world of leadership, she has been a constant presence, and has remained right by my side.

When I asked Mrs. Roth if she would consider contributing to my book, her affirmative response felt like the most special "yes" I had ever received. As a ten-year-old in her classroom, it was beyond my wildest dreams that I would one day author a book, much less include my favorite teacher in it. After extensive discussions about her contribution, we decided to craft our narrative as a back-and-forth exchange. I hope you find joy and inspiration in the unique dialogue that unfolds.

> I'll never forget the day I walked into her classroom. Although I was only nine years old, I can still remember thinking that she was one of the most innovative and inspiring teachers I'd ever had. She had this unbelievable ability to lead with empathy, ensuring you felt special and valued. She celebrated your strengths, asked you to share them with peers, made learning incredibly fun, and continuously implemented new and better teaching and learning practices. The overhead projector (remember those?) was a staple in her practice when most other teachers had them pushed into a corner in the back of the room (perhaps because it was a new and unfamiliar technological tool). I didn't realize it then, but she used it to model her own writing life, make her invisible thinking visible, and show us "the learning process" across various content areas. I often replay the images in my mind to re-create the memories. It goes something like this: Me, lovingly staring at her with my elbows locked on my desk and the palms of my hands cupping my chin as she gracefully carried around a book that was practically stuck to her hands like glue. This book looked important because it had that "lived-in" look about it. It was worn out at the edges, like it had been thumbed through frequently, had colored tabs strategically placed throughout, and

> was covered with intentional highlighting, underlined words, phrases, and sentences from top to bottom. It was a book that reminded me of my favorite "go-to" '80s movies—you know, the ones I watched over and over again because I connected with the plot lines and hidden gems of life lessons, or the humorous parts that made me laugh or the serious parts that got me to reflect on my own life and all the "what if this happened to me?" moments!
>
> — LAUREN

It was the Monday after Labor Day—signaling the start of a new school year. My summer had been a mix of relaxation, enjoying time with friends and family, and refining and crafting a curriculum that would engage and inspire students to foster a love of learning. During this time, I delved into *In the Middle* by Nancie Atwell, a book that held promises for fresh approaches to teaching literacy. My enthusiasm brimmed as I couldn't wait to embed some of the suggestions into my own instructional practices. Filled with joy at the thought of meeting my new students, I wanted to ensure that my classroom was warm and welcoming as I was ready to embark on a journey of growth and discovery together with them.

And then the day came—the students arrived, eager to begin a new year! Through a series of intentional introductions, I got a sense of the various cultural backgrounds, family structures, and life experiences that made up our class. Each student possessed unique talents and interests, creating the most dynamic learning environment. As the new school year progressed, a particular student caught my attention for so many reasons—Lauren. From the moment she stepped into the classroom, her infectious warmth and genuine kindness were evident. With a natural teacher's heart, she had the ability to make everyone feel valued and included, bringing a sense of unity to the classroom. Her compassion for others left a deep impact, becoming a source of inspiration to myself and others in her orbit. It was because of Lauren's love for learning that she displayed the innate ability to coach, encourage, and inspire others. Throughout the school year, little did I know that Lauren would forge lasting bonds that extended far beyond the classroom walls, forming an especially enduring connection with me.

———— LINDA ————

I contemplated asking Mrs. Roth the name of the treasured book she walked around with, but I was a painfully shy young girl, so shy that I only spoke in class when I was invited to do so. Also, was it appropriate for an elementary student to be interested in a grown-up resource for teachers? And then what I thought was the perfect moment arrived, my lucky day. I noticed that the mysterious, treasured book was left by itself on the kidney-shaped table Mrs. Roth used for small group instruction. I spontaneously grabbed my notebook and pencil, briskly walked up to the table, and furiously scribbled down the title and author of the book. This was all while Mrs. Roth wrote the schedule for the day on the chalkboard in different-colored chalk. I hurried back to my desk and immediately opened my notebook to read the title: *In the Middle: A Lifetime of Learning about Writing, Reading, and Adolescents* by Nancie Atwell. I thought, *So, this is the book that Mrs. Roth kept close to her teaching heart.* I had to have it! I felt compelled to emulate the qualities I saw in Mrs. Roth, someone who valued her students, who created exciting learning experiences, who made you feel like your contributions mattered and kept you running back to school every day. And, if I was going to be a teacher one day, I wanted to be the teacher that felt empowered to create innovative experiences for students and colleagues. I wanted to be the teacher who was collegial, but also not afraid of success or the idea of positively impacting others in dynamic, influential ways. I wanted to be that teacher who embraced every student and tapped into their passions and interests. I wanted to be the teacher who was aware of the learning goals by offering students various pathways to showcase their learning. I wanted to value people and creativity, and motivate others to share their gifts. So, at the age of nine years old, I asked my parents if they would purchase the book for me, and they did.

— LAUREN —

I cherished my teaching journey and embraced its noble path. I deeply appreciated the opportunity to shape students' lives and create meaningful experiences that could influence their future. Sharing and exchanging ideas with colleagues was invigorating; it fueled me to hold onto a steadfast commitment to lifelong professional learning, staying on the forefront of education. As I actively participated in committees with bright administrators, my own dreams of pursuing leadership lit a spark within me. My love for my career must have caught the attention of an upper-level administrator who encouraged me to pursue my administration degree. I'll never forget the words a particular mentor imparted: "Your enthusiasm for learning and growth is infectious with children and would be equally infectious with administrators. You are ready for this leap, and I know you would foster a culture of continuous improvement. Imagine the satisfaction of seeing the results of your efforts reflected in the success of an entire school community!" It felt great to be noticed and validated by a strong, well-respected leader. Eagerly, I enrolled to obtain my administrator credentials, invigorated by the uncharted opportunities of entering the realm of administration.

Throughout my educational and administrative careers, the presence of exceptional mentors propelled my personal success as a leader. Each mentoring partnership provided me with invaluable guidance and unwavering support and allowed me to navigate challenges and make informed decisions. Their guidance expedited my learning curve, enabling me to accelerate my leadership abilities, capitalize on future opportunities, set higher goals, and strive for excellence. Through my many mentors, I was exposed to a greater networking field, which opened new doors, enriching my professional landscape.

Following my first appointment as an assistant principal, other doors began to open as I ascended the ladder and became a curriculum director, and assistant superintendent for curriculum and instruction. Although my mentors stayed with me as I grew as a leader, with time, roles shifted, and *I* assumed the role of a mentor. The most impactful mentoring relationships I encountered on my path were enduring, dynamic, and reciprocal in nature. Cultivating robust and meaningful relationships enriches the vitality that each of us carries forward, propelling us into a state of collective effervescence. Now, after a forty-year career, I clearly believe that the unwritten responsibility of leadership is to notice and uplift excellence in others, to create environments where every educator and leader reaches their personal best.

—— LINDA ——

And so, when I assumed the role of instructional coach, Mrs. Karen Sauter, my principal and cooperating administrator, shared the following sentiment: "Now, you are going to have to get your administrative credential, Lauren. That's your next step—leadership. You are a leader." As I pursued my certification, Mrs. Roth's voice often lingered in my eternal mental movie, her voice echoing within, and I thought, *What advice would Mrs. Roth offer in this scenario? How would she navigate this?* After all, she culminated her career as

> a central office administrator; she must have held a treasure trove of experiences that could be shared with an aspiring leader like myself. Upon completing my certification and embarking on the quest for administrative roles, I chose not to think further; instead, I dialed her number. "Mrs. Roth, I'm pursuing administrative positions and would be immensely grateful for your guidance," I confided. Her response was heartening: "Lauren, mentoring you would be my privilege."
>
> — LAUREN

> Upon reconnecting, Lauren had evolved into a seasoned educator, characterized by her intelligence, eloquence, and adept interpersonal skills. Her mastery of teaching was evident, often shared through inspiring stories of guiding others to realize their potential. Our discussions centered on her aspirations for administrative roles, where she could leverage her talents effectively. Navigating interviews tests both professional competence and emotional resilience. Lauren faced rejections for positions she had applied for, prompting doubt. As her mentor, I encouraged her to persist, even when she hit a low point. With reluctance, she agreed to one more interview, a decision that proved pivotal.
>
> — LINDA

> The interviewing process is an emotional roller coaster, where excitement, anticipation, and nerves intertwine. Sometimes, I received those encouraging "taps on the shoulder," while at other times, I ventured forward independently. While serving in my previous school district, there were a few leaders who stood by my side and wanted to help me secure a position whenever and however they could. That made me feel special and valued. "Lauren, allow me to send your résumé into that school district,

allow me to write you a recommendation, or make that phone call on your behalf." Sometimes, I took them up on it; how could I not? How kind and supportive of these leaders who truly believed in me.

Having reached the final stages with a few districts after enduring exhaustive processes involving various stakeholder groups, the sting of receiving rejection calls was sometimes overwhelming. I felt my passion for education begin to waver, and I questioned my aspirations. One particular interview stands out in my memory—one where I didn't even progress beyond the initial screening. I eagerly accepted an offer of feedback from a central office administrator. His words cut through: "Lauren, you didn't talk about the kids!" Perplexed and aggravated with myself, I called Linda, immediately recounting the situation. The absurdity of not discussing my core focus left us both in a state of shock and then instant laughter.

A moment arrived when I contemplated quitting the entire process. The disappointments left my spirit diminished, demanding time to mend. "One more, Lauren, just one more! PLEASE," Linda begged. Reluctantly, I agreed to one final attempt. Miraculously, that attempt turned out to be the breakthrough I needed—the pivotal one that led to success. Suddenly, I was embarking on my first formal leadership role as an assistant principal.

— LAUREN —

One of my greatest joys is being a mentor to Lauren. I see my younger self in her. I have watched Lauren traverse and navigate a multitude of landscapes. The very qualities Lauren possessed as a nine-year-old student in my class, she possesses now. There is a magic that unfolds when two educators with a shared passion for teaching form an invisible bond. There is a remarkable twist

> of fate when two educators, separated by a span of thirty years, find themselves bound by parallel stories that transcend time. The exchange of stories, successes, and challenges deepens the connection. Throughout the mentor/mentee relationship, each is reminded of the purpose that led them to be educators. Each is passionate about and committed to making a difference in the lives of students and the greater educational community.
>
> — LINDA

## When the Past Meets the Present

Over a decade ago, one of my previous supervisors sent an email inviting a group of literacy teachers to attend a Nancie Atwell conference. I immediately jumped on the opportunity to meet the literacy expert who had a profound impact on my favorite teacher, and me. Before leaving for the early morning New York City conference, I tucked my "lived-in," worn at the edges, highlighted, underlined, tab-filled twenty-one-year-old *In the Middle: A Lifetime of Learning about Writing, Reading, and Adolescents* book in my bag. As I listened to Atwell speak about her passion for literacy and what it means to her to empower learners to have meaningful literacy lives, I couldn't help but think about what got me to that moment. If it wasn't for Mrs. Roth, her love for learning, and empowering her learners to grow, would I be sitting at the table with other educators who had traveled near and far for a Saturday morning of professional learning?

During the lunch break, I patiently waited for my turn to speak with Nancie Atwell and held my adored book in hand. I got to share the story about why and how I have a twenty-one-year-old copy of the book. She smiled, laughed, and appeared to have connected with my experience. Then, she looked a bit stunned. "Wait a minute, your parents bought you my book when you were in fourth grade?" She graciously and immediately signed my precious copy, a cherished book that symbolizes eternal memories that manifest hope for the future.

Throughout my educational journey, Mrs. Roth remained a constant presence in my thoughts. I often pondered how she charted her career's course and summoned the courage to embrace leadership. There was a time in my professional path that leaving the classroom seemed inconceivable. After all, what other role could instill a true legacy within the hearts and minds of the students we guide?

*Do you ever find yourself continuously reflecting on the impact your mentors have had on your growth and development both personally and professionally?* Such retrospection, I believe, rekindles the flame of purpose. Just imagine if every child encountered their own guiding light like my own, Mrs. Roth. *How would having these positive role models impact their personal journeys, encourage them to create their own opportunities, and then share those gifts with the world?*

## A note to Linda Roth (my teacher and mentor):

I feel incredibly lucky to have my fourth-grade teacher in my life. After over thirty years of losing touch, we were not only able to pick up where we left off, but our relationship evolved into one of thought partners who have a mutual respect for one another. As I write this portion of the chapter, Linda will have not seen the message below until she picks up the book with you.

*Dear Linda (Mrs. Roth),*

*In the tapestry of our lives, the threads of past and present have a funny way of intersecting. Thank you for taking my call after all these years. Just like when I was a child, you are still here for me when I need you the most. By writing this chapter together, we were able to bridge the past with the present, weaving a story of growth, inspiration, and connection. Along our respective career paths, we have discovered that educators, mentors, and leaders have the power to leave lasting impressions that resonate across*

# The Leader Inside

time, instilling belief, resilience, and growth. Our story is unique and highlights an enduring bond that transcends decades.

You have illuminated my path and guided me through uncertainty and celebrations. You have empowered me to lead through an empathetic lens. I know I am not perfect, I will make mistakes throughout the rest of my journey, but I know that I can persevere hearing your voice in my mind and your encouragement in my heart. Our relationship reminds me that our influence extends far beyond titles; it resides in the hearts and minds of those we touch. Our legacies are etched not in stone but in the stories we share, the connections we forge, and the vulnerabilities we embrace.

Thank you for helping me discover the leader inside. I love you.

With gratitude and admiration,
Lauren

Linda Roth, my dad, Bob Epstein, and fourth-grade Lauren

## Actionable Ideas to Implement Tomorrow

All learners deserve to meet trusted people who will be their champions. All learners deserve to be welcomed into an environment that values their stories. All learners deserve to have a voice and choice in how they learn. All learners could use an invitation to share their thinking in safe spaces. All learners should have the opportunity to pay attention to the books and practices their teachers employ to bring out the very best within them.

In what manner do you aspire to etch your legacy as an educator, leaving an indelible mark on the students you guide and the colleagues you collaborate with?

To strive for such an impactful legacy as an educator, consider the following:

- **Cultivate Enduring Mentorship:** Educators and leaders should actively seek out mentorship relationships to guide their professional growth. Mentorship offers invaluable guidance, accelerates learning curves, and propels personal and career development.
  **Reflective Question:** How can you initiate or enhance a mentoring relationship to endure and support your growth as an educator or leader?
- **Create Inviting Learning Environments:** Establish classrooms where each student feels valued and empowered. Encourage students to share their unique strengths and interests, promoting a sense of unity and inclusion among a variety of backgrounds.
  **Reflective Question:** How can you create a sense of belonging that honors and celebrates the many talents and backgrounds of your students?
- **Elevate Interview Preparedness through Storytelling:** Enhance your interview performance by incorporating compelling stories that showcase your passion, experience, and commitment to education. Craft anecdotes that align with the qualities and skills desired for the position.

**Reflective Question:** What significant experiences can you transform into impactful stories that effectively communicate your qualifications during interviews?

- **Express Your Gratitude:** Take a moment to write a heartfelt letter of gratitude to a person who has inspired your educational or professional journey. Share how their guidance and support have impacted your growth and development.

**Reflective Question:** How can the act of expressing gratitude not only acknowledge the impact of others but also deepen your own sense of connection and purpose in your journey?

**Meghan Lawson** is the author of *Legacy of Learning: Teaching for Lasting Impact* and a thought leader who studies and implements the conditions and systems needed for transformational change. A lover of learning who believes in the goodness of people, Meghan works to cultivate necessary space that honors the humanity of all people. She promotes  storytelling, the exchange of ideas, and risk-taking. She is passionate about disrupting the status quo and creating kinder, forward-thinking communities of action. Meghan is also intensely curious about how to enhance the customer experience in schools. Meghan began her career in the English language arts classroom. So, inevitably, her mantra is "Words matter." In her eighteen-plus years in the field of education, she has worked in all levels of K–12 education as a teacher, school administrator, district administrator, and educational consultant. You can connect with Meghan on X (@meghan_lawson), on Instagram (@meghanlawsonblog), or on her blog at meghanlawson.com.

CHAPTER TWELVE

# Be Your Own Champion

## BY MEGHAN LAWSON

> *The universe buries strange jewels deep within us all, and then stands back to see if we can find them.*
>
> —ELIZABETH GILBERT, *BIG MAGIC*

### Learn, Unlearn, Relearn

When I look back, many of the important lessons I've uncovered about leadership come from my time as a middle school teacher. Middle school students are fun, fascinating, and challenging to teach because they show up in so many different places developmentally. As a middle school ELA teacher, I learned how to be a resilient action practitioner. When an instructional approach didn't work with some of my students, I learned to become curious about why, and to try again without allowing failures to be internalized as reflections of my worth as a human being or teacher. This took practice on my part. I think I shed more tears after school as a middle school teacher than I have in any other role. Learning how to be a good teacher is hard work, and it's made even harder when we put unrealistic expectations on ourselves. How we talk to ourselves is critical to our success, stamina, and longevity in this beautiful profession. This is why it is also vital that we surround ourselves with people who see our potential to grow and expand into the biggest, best versions of ourselves.

My principal at the time, Dr. Kimberly P. Miller, held high expectations for staff and supported us in achieving those expectations. I can still remember her weekly visits to my classroom. While she was kind and disarming, she often asked a thoughtful question or shared a reflection in those moments that made me want to work harder or try something new. She modeled being a learner as well as what it looked like to be curious about learners and their learning experience. I was honored when she asked me to be the English language arts department leader after working with her for a couple of years. Looking back, I'm pretty confident no one else wanted the job, haha, but she made me feel capable and empowered, especially as a young woman still early in my teaching career.

I think this was my first experience where a principal made space in meetings for learning. We read books and articles and talked about them at our monthly building leadership team meetings. I looked forward to the dialogue and was enamored with becoming more knowledgeable and effective in my classroom. While success is not solely measured by test scores or one data point, my state test data indicated that the shifts in my instructional practices were leading to gains in student growth and achievement.

When I first started at the school, I had taught high school English for four years. The transition to teaching middle school proved more challenging than I had anticipated. They weren't just "younger versions of high school students." Many of my go-to strategies were proving ineffective, and my data showed it. My student growth on the state assessment was in the red after that first year, and I had a choice. I could either allow that to inspire my growth and development or be crushed. Kim maintained high expectations and supported me on my path to improvement. In that second year, my scores were in the yellow, indicating that my students maintained expected growth. I was encouraged that the instructional changes I was making were working. That third year, I joined the building leadership team. As I mentioned, we read books, enjoyed dialogue about the art and science of teaching, and tried research-supported instructional practices in our classrooms. Specifically, we focused on formative instructional practices. I can still remember Kim asking me, "Will all of your students pass the state assessment this school year?" To which I replied, "I hope they do!" with a spirit of underpromise and overdeliver. She countered without missing a beat, "Hope is not a strategy." That year, all of my students, including one who had not earned a proficient score on a state assessment in over two years, passed the test. My student growth was in the green, exceeding expectations.

I recently ran into Kim at the BASA Women in Leadership Conference, where I was leading a session. I can remember exactly where we were standing in the hallway when she said something like, "I am so proud of you. I always knew you were going to do great things, but you've exceeded what I imagined." I cried tears of pride on my drive home. I'm a forty-year-old woman, and still that kind of encouragement from someone you deeply admired as a teacher your heart strongly. Kim also attended the session I led that day. As part of the session, I unpacked some of the hope research shared by Jamie Meade, vice president and chief of staff for Battelle for Kids. As Meade explains, according to the research of C. S. Snyder, "Hope is a more robust predictor of future success than SAT, ACT, or GPA."[46] It turns out that hope is not a feeling but more like a muscle we can strengthen that can deeply impact our future success and that of our students.

## Hope IS a Strategy

Kim joked with me after the session, "Remember when I used to say that hope is not a strategy?" I smiled, knowing what was coming next. "Guess I was wrong." We both laughed. I share that to show that great leaders admit when they are wrong. They allow new information to be considered and give themselves the freedom to change their minds when they know better. I hope to continue to learn, relearn, and unlearn and to model this for others. If we never allow ourselves to rethink, how can we ever get better? The future of our children depends on our commitment to our own growth and development and that of others. We are literally in the learning business, and one of the best ways to cultivate and inspire learning in others is to cultivate and inspire learning within ourselves.

During my time on the leadership team with Kim, I remember staying back for a few minutes one day when we were both cleaning up after a meeting. I can remember exactly where I was sitting in the room and where she was standing when she said, "Have you ever thought about becoming a principal?" I was shocked and honored by the question. Uncomfortable, I quipped back, "Why would I ever want to do your job? Your job looks terrible." She laughed, acknowledging that there are certainly difficult aspects to the job, but she told me that being an administrator could give me an opportunity to expand my impact beyond the classroom. Certainly, this is not the only way to expand our impact, but it is one way. I thought about it more and found myself sitting up a bit more confidently. She saw me as someone capable of taking on that kind of responsibility.

That fall, I started my coursework and the next school year, I started a job as assistant principal of a neighboring middle school. Since then, I've had the opportunity to be an elementary principal, a district administrator, and an educational consultant. My passion for learning and growing has led me to become a contributing author, and to write my very own book, *Legacy of Learning: Teaching for Lasting Impact*. I don't know that twenty-eight-year-old me would have believed it. Never say never, right? The titles have never mattered much to me. The "power" has never mattered to me. It's the opportunity to empower and expand how others view themselves and their ability to make a difference that matters to me. I know what it feels like to have someone see something in you that you didn't see in yourself. And I've seen that I am more capable and stronger than I ever imagined.

Many of us as women wait to take on opportunities when we are 100 percent ready. We will never be 100 percent ready. So, when other women show us that we know enough to start and are capable of figuring out the rest as we go, that is life-giving. When other women show us what it looks like to do the work competently but imperfectly, it gives us an opportunity to look at ourselves and think, *Well, maybe I could do that!* Perhaps this is why I'm deeply committed to being authentically myself and deeply human in front of others. If we do not share our mistakes and our learnings with others, we make these jobs something that only perfect people, or perfect women, do. There are no perfect people or perfect women. The future of learning, school, our world, depends on our ability to inspire other people to grow and expand into their best work and best selves. If they see leading classrooms, schools, districts, or organizations as something only perfect people do, they cannot imagine a future for themselves in these roles. We don't need more perfect, shiny women leading. We need deeply human women who center the humanity of others in the learning process.

## The Story of Us

While I've experienced my fair share of setbacks and there have been times I was underestimated or overlooked, I know some of my greatest limitations as a female in leadership are the ones I've placed on myself. I have doubted myself, my skills, and my capabilities. This is not just my story. It's the story of us. Many women do this. Which is why it is mission critical that we encourage and nourish the hearts and minds of other women, helping them to see their potential when they can't see it for themselves. It is also why it's important that we learn to be our own champions and have our own backs. There is one voice that never leaves us, and that is our own voice. We must learn to speak to ourselves the way we would speak to someone we love dearly. We can hold space for our feelings, and maintain high expectations for our own learning and performance. When we make mistakes, which we certainly will if we are working on anything worth doing, we can learn to encourage ourselves to try and try again without losing confidence in our capabilities. We can do all of this with what Brené Brown describes as a "Strong back. Soft front. Wild heart."[47] Meaning, we can do hard things without allowing it to harden us as human beings. We can do hard things without losing our sense of play, our joy, and our adventure. In fact, I would argue that our joy, our play, and our sense of adventure are what make the work smarter, more creative, and more alive.

I'm sure there are people who don't take me very seriously at first because of my pink remote keyboard or because I wear sequin sneakers to work or because I write with feather flamingo pens. There are people who have said that I'm "just a pretty face who makes people feel good." There are people who think that I'm all good snacks and fun music at meetings and positive Post-it notes. And when people are committed to misunderstanding me, I let them. It's not my job to make them believe differently. My job is to do my best work and to show up as my best self and to continue learning and growing. My work stands for itself and over time, when it really matters, people come around and realize that there is more to me and my impact. For a long time, I let the misunderstandings bother me. But now, it's kind of fun proving people wrong. I've done "big scary things," but I don't do them because they are big and scary. I do them when I know it's the right thing to do. Just because I smile and carry it well, doesn't mean it's not heavy. It simply means that I choose joy because I do my best work when I'm in a more positive mental space. This does not mean that I ignore hard truths. This does not mean that I don't make space for others and their big feelings. This does not mean that I don't struggle or share in those struggles. This simply means that when I feel better, my work gets better, and I hope to make that same impact on others. As Shawn Achor says, "Our brains at positive are 31 percent more productive than they are at negative, neutral, or stressed.[48] This number, 31 percent, is significant, and I hope to be someone who nourishes the conditions necessary for others to tap into their 31 percent.

Thankfully, Kim was willing to invest in my learning and grow her impact by growing my belief in myself and my capabilities. I cannot think of a more meaningful legacy than to do the same for others. Isn't that what we all got into education to do? To grow hearts and minds?

There is a quiet whisper in your heart. A call for something more. Please allow this book to affirm for you whatever it may be, you can do it. You've got this. Now go be your own champion.

## Actionable Ideas to Implement Tomorrow

Oprah once said, "Don't worry about being 'successful.' Strive for the truest, highest expression of yourself . . . and then use that expression in service to the world. If the paradigm for which you see the world is, 'How can I be of service with my talent? How can I be used in service?' then I guarantee you, no matter what your talent or offering, you will be successful."

- Quite simply, when do you feel the most yourself and the most alive in your work?
- What conditions were in place that nourished your work in this way, and how might you create more of that for yourself and/or others?
- How might you utilize the work that makes you feel alive to deepen your impact on others?

MOVING FORWARD

# Your Impact Moves with You

## BY LAUREN M. KAUFMAN

> *Courage starts with showing up and letting ourselves be seen.*
>
> —BRENÉ BROWN

### Bridging the Past and the Future

I thought I would retire in the last district I served in. It was close to where I live, a district I loved, a place I called home. I remember the day I realized that I needed to move on so I could grow into the leader and educator I was meant to become. After going through a handful of interview processes and some disappointments, I was offered an assistant principal role in the right place, at the right time, with the people I was destined to know.

I was set to embark on this exciting new endeavor in the middle of summer. So, a hot end-of-July day was the last time I'd use my ID fob to enter a building in a district I adored for so long. It's where I evolved as an instructional coach and reading specialist. That day, I filled fifteen boxes with treasured stories from my teaching past. I looked around the empty classroom, only leaving behind the books that belonged to the school. When I was ready to go, I peeked my head out the door to look for a custodial staff member to help me find a flatbed wagon and help lift and stack my boxes and bring them to my car. Oddly, there was no one in sight. After a brief search, I found a flatbed myself. I closed my eyes, taking a deep breath and putting my AirPods into my ears because to me, what is life without music, especially during a pivotal moment like this? My iTunes randomly played "High Hopes" by Panic! At The Disco. It seemed fitting, the perfect song for the symbolic transition from teaching to leadership. I tied back my hair, loaded my boxes onto the flatbed, and as sweat dripped from my brow, I pulled this big, heavy flatbed wagon out to my car. I opened my trunk, pushed down all the seats, and lifted each box one by one, finally filling my trunk to the brim. I took a picture to capture the moment, the end of an era.

Boxing up my teaching days, ready to embark on a journey to a new chapter.

When I drove off that day, I thought about all the small moments that led me to this new opportunity in leadership. I thought about some of the lessons I'd learned from leaders, colleagues, and students. I thought about the happiness, the joy, the laughter, the comradery of teachers, some sadness and disappointment, the evolution of me, and all the small moments that brought me to this place in time.

The next day I pulled up to a new building, my new home, where I was greeted by Mario, the friendly head custodian. He met me by my car and helped me unload my trunk of boxes, the treasured stories of the educator I was. His genuine smile gave me the courage I needed to retrieve my new ID fob from my bag, swipe it at a new door, and step toward the unforeseen lessons I would learn on the path to the leader I hoped to become.

As I reflected on the final year I had a classroom to call my own, little did I imagine that the subsequent year would lead me to embrace a formal leadership role amid a pandemic—one of the most challenging periods in educational history. For five years prior, I had cherished my role as an instructional coach, and I never anticipated that it would be dissolved for various reasons. Faced with this change and drawing from my extensive experience in elementary education spanning over a decade, I decided to transition to the middle school as a literacy specialist for students in grades six through eight. Embracing new challenges has always been integral to my growth as a human being, educator, learner, leader, and practitioner. It is through these endeavors that I strive to remain at the cutting edge of best practices, enhance my skill set, and uplift others.

The excitement of sharing the wealth of knowledge I had accumulated in diverse settings filled my thoughts. Yet, little did I know that this endeavor would require me to navigate physical and virtual spaces simultaneously, forever altering my perception of the role and impact of teachers. As I embarked on this journey, I cherished every opportunity to impart my learning and contribute to the growth of young minds. I hold dear the memories of my own classroom, knowing that this chapter marks the end of a remarkable era in my educational journey. However, it also signified the beginning of new opportunities to empower and inspire as I continue to evolve as an educator and leader.

The trajectory of my career has been a journey filled with unexpected surprises, leading me to places I could have never anticipated or imagined. My purpose of bringing out the gifts in others while keeping kids at the heart of decision-making has always remained steadfast. However, every path I've walked has presented me with a collection of choices that have forced me to summon the momentum inside myself to take action and acknowledge that growth and comfort cannot coexist.

## Embracing Imperfection

I have to admit that early on in my career, I found myself spending time dwelling on how things are supposed to be. I lived by rules that were influenced by traditional norms and the ones I created for myself, striving to row toward a place of perfection, and waiting for the right moment to start something new. I told myself that the conditions needed to feel "right," more trust needed to be established, or that I needed to strengthen my knowledge base before I could take action. However, the days of perseverating over shiny plans and methods have been long done. What I have learned is that stepping into the mess of learning, focusing on priorities and outcomes, embracing what is actually in front of me, paying attention to what feels right, and letting life unfold is the key to moving toward where I am meant to be.

So I ask, *How can leaders let go of preconceived expectations, embrace the transformative process of continuous learning, and forge a path that aligns with where they are meant to be?*

In the 2021–2022 school year, I embarked on my first administrative role as an assistant principal in a wonderful school district. From the moment I stepped into the building, I was greeted by kids and colleagues running up to me, knowing my name, and eager to share their excitement about the day ahead. It felt incredible to have an opportunity to be a part of something so much bigger than myself. I have never taken for granted that I was entrusted to lead, learn, and grow into a leadership role. With the support of an amazing principal who served as a role model during what was considered one of the hardest years in education, I dove headfirst into the experience. I loved learning about the assistant principal role, which is heavily rooted in student life, connecting with students, families, the administrative team, and fellow educators. There is something unbelievably special about being a building administrator. Every day you get to strengthen connections to the people around you. You make an impact on the hearts and minds of those you serve, in the same place, every day. It's like having a built-in family and a consistent place to call home. Of course, there are challenges, and my biggest learning curve was understanding the day-to-day operations of the building and navigating safety protocols.

Just as I was hitting my stride as an assistant principal and feeling more confident in my ability to build relationships and drive instructional improvement, there was an opportunity to become the director of literacy K–12. At first, the idea of leaving behind the school community that had become so meaningful to me didn't feel right. In one year, I had poured so much of myself into building relationships with students, teachers, and families, and I wasn't sure I was ready to give that up. Nonetheless, the opportunity to make a broader impact on literacy instruction across the district and strengthen learning experiences for kids felt incredibly important. As I reflected on the bigger picture, I began to see my internal obstacle as a chance to open a door to a new path. Ultimately, I decided to take a leap of faith, embracing the new challenge set before me, even though it meant leaving behind a role that had come to feel so rewarding.

## Cultures of Learning Are Built on Connection

Recently, I took a trip to Los Angeles, California. I go there every summer to reconnect with friends in a place I spent a lot of time in in my early twenties. Since I had a very early flight, I made a last minute decision to take an Uber to the airport. My pickup time was 4:45 a.m. (sigh). I can still remember my eyes feeling heavy when I received a message from my driver. I looked at my iPhone and it was 4:30 a.m. The message read, "Hi Lauren, I'm here and ready when you are." *Wow*, I thought. All my anxiety about making that early flight completely vanished. When I opened the car door and greeted my driver, Sierra, the first thing I saw was her sincere and warm smile. "Good morning, Lauren. I wanted to get here nice and early so you didn't have to worry." I smiled through my relieved response and addressed this Uber driver I had now known for thirty seconds by name, "How thoughtful of you, Sierra. Thank you so much. May I have this cup of coffee in your car?" Sierra laughed. "Well, I wouldn't have been here this early if I wasn't on my second cup. Of course, Lauren, if you didn't have a cup with you, I would have asked if you'd like me to stop for one." I had only known Sierra for a few minutes, but her caring gesture and curiosity in getting to know me as a human being made me feel safe and reassured that I would make it to my flight without a hitch, creating an instant connection between us.

Although I will most likely never see Sierra again, this encounter reminded me of a profound lesson about education. I realized that my vast knowledge as a literacy educator would hold little significance to my students unless I could foster genuine connections with them. They weren't solely interested in my expertise; they were curious about who I was, who I am, and who I aspired to be. Similarly, I discovered that to cultivate a culture of learning, communication, collaboration, and empowerment in the classroom, I needed to invest in my students' hearts and find the leaders living inside them. It wasn't just about delivering content; it was about getting to know my students, understanding their aspirations, and supporting them on their unique journeys of growth and development. By showcasing my authentic self and investing in meaningful connections with my students, I found the key to building a truly impactful educational experience.

## Small Moves, Big Impact

In the book Legacy of Learning: Teaching for Last Impact by Meghan Lawson, I share the following, "There will be small moments, small wins, and small obstacles on the path that can seem like they are not enough to bring a vision to fruition. But they add up to the big things that we truly need to accomplish."[49] Have you ever thought about how your personal evolution and the path to the educator you are becoming exists in the small things? *Where are you now and where do you want to be?* Happiness doesn't just exist in where we are, it lives in what we do to get there. Just three years ago, you would have found me in a classroom teaching reading to sixth- to eighth-grade students in the midst of a pandemic. Now, I am grateful to serve as a building and district leader, which has led me to working with a new team, students, and community. Although my roles have changed, I am the same person at the core. I have the same heart and passion for what I do. I recognize that it's the small things that have contributed to endless refinement and continuous improvement toward the educator I am becoming. It's the small things that have illuminated my love for education and the constant pursuit to be better for the people I serve.

You see, it's the small wins that add up to the big things. When you love what you do, you have the motivation to remain courageous in your convictions. Even the setbacks you experience have the potential to become aha moments that fuel new ideas and catapult your drive for the person you wish to become. It's the small things that pave the way to the big things. It could be the people you meet along the way; they may have taken the time to listen to your dreams, your ideas, and validate what you believe in and what you stand for. Those are the same people who probably told you, "You can." Those small things may have been a smile, a nod, a note, a glimmer of encouragement, a push into pursuing opportunities you didn't know were waiting for you. Those small things may have helped you say yes to yourself and encouraged you to shatter the walls of fear as you were fervently finding your way. Maybe that small thing was someone who used the words "No, you can't." Thank that person for that; this was your opportunity to embrace every ounce of self-doubt to ignite determination and hope on the road to achieving personal growth.

Small moves breathe new meaning into a year. In his book *Atomic Habits*, James Clear says, "We often dismiss small changes because they don't seem to matter much in the moment."[50] Looking back, there were a lot of small things I didn't savor in the moment. It's the small things that led me to the place I am today; they are rooted in a collection of interactions I've had with people, family, friends, students, and colleagues. The gradual evolution of becoming yourself is wrapped up in small things that happen over time. My friend, educational leader and author Sean Gaillard, recently shared a small thing, a simple sentiment in an X post: "Consider the possibilities." Take a moment to look beyond your immediate surroundings—look for the small things in new people and possibilities on the horizon. *Where are you now, and where do you want to be in a year?*

On one of my last days in the classroom, I read my students *Only One You* by Linda Kranz. The book inspired me to use all I had learned about my students and write them a personal note of inspiration and gratitude. With that, I also left them a special rock with the one word I felt embodied who they are and who they will continue to be. I remember my student Steven picking up his rock "Happiness" and studying it carefully. "Mrs. Kaufman, do you really think I can bring happiness to people wherever I go?" he asked. I replied, "Steven, your happiness is contagious and will bring joy to whomever you meet. Your happiness will change the world."

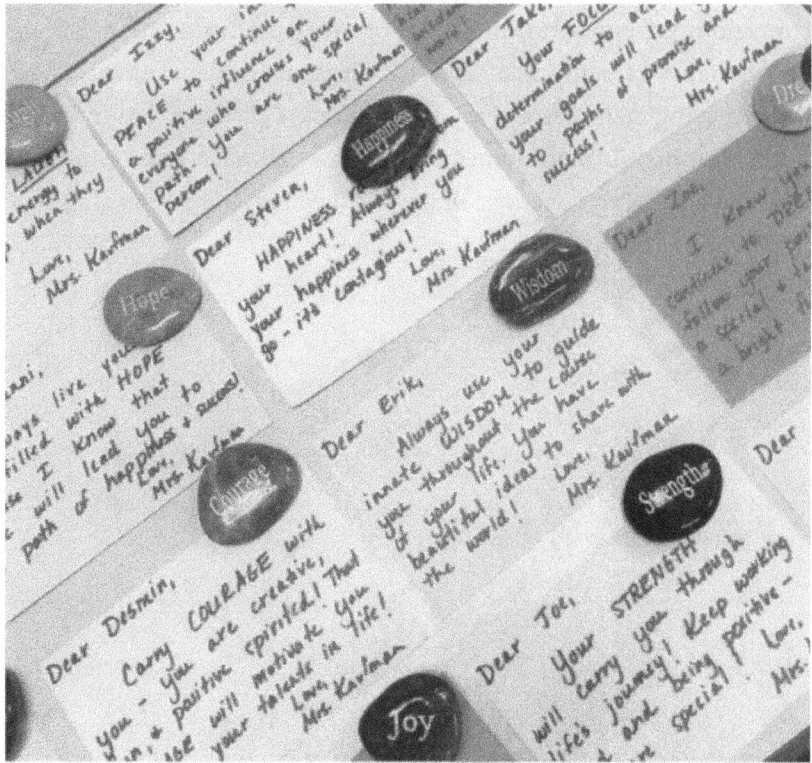

Leaving behind personalized notes and small tokens for my students on my final day of teaching.

And just like that, it's a few years later, and I am proudly serving as a district leader with a new team of people I was destined to know. The last interaction I had with Steven was just one moment in the collection of small moves I employed that would later influence the school leader I am learning to become. I often reflect on the small moves I am choosing to make to connect with people. One of the best parts of my new role is visiting classrooms to spend time with students and teachers. Recently, a student named James delightfully approached me with a piece of writing he wanted to share. One sentiment he included was, "When you walk by, say hi to Mrs. Kaufman. Don't you want to make her day? Mrs. Kaufman is wonderful because she makes sure everyone has a good day." As I read James's piece of writing, it brought me back to the exchange I had with Steven. It made me think about how Steven's contagious happiness became a part of me. It seemed as though I was inadvertently bringing that same happiness to James. Perhaps I have been carrying many years of my students' and colleagues' positive attributes with me. At that moment, I asked myself, *How can we continuously recognize that a collection of small actions have the potential to make someone else's day better?*

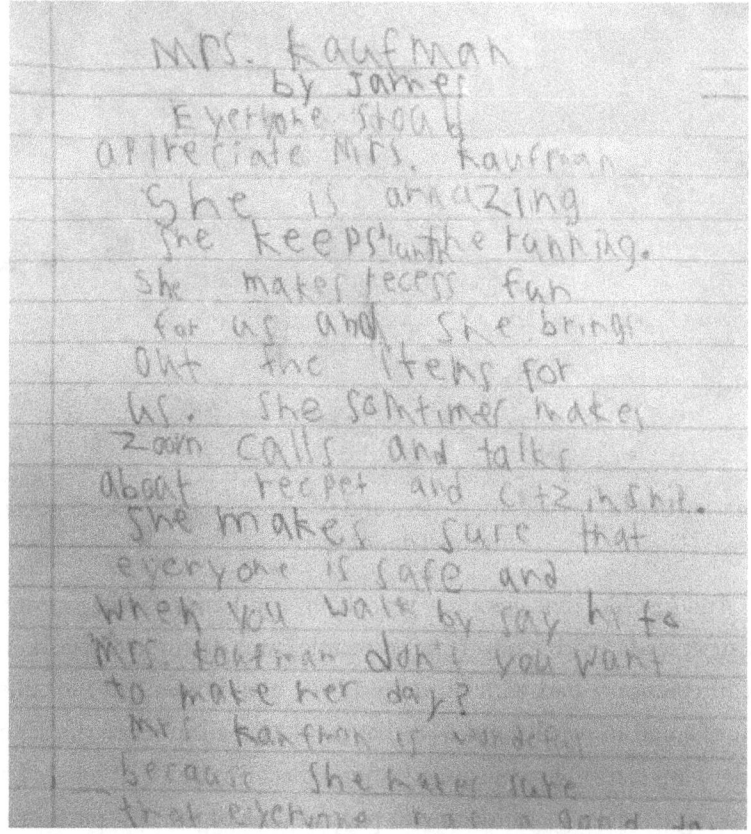

A heartwarming surprise note from a student named James during my time as an assistant principal.

*Everyone should appreciate Mrs. Kaufman. She keeps the lunch running. She makes recess fun for us and she brings out the items for us. She sometimes makes Zoom calls and talks about respect and citizenship. She makes sure that everyone is safe and when you walk by, say hi to Mrs. Kaufman. Don't you want to make her day? Mrs. Kaufman is wonderful because she makes sure that everyone has a good day. –James (2nd-grade student)*

## Who Is the Leader You Wish to Become?

As a passionate educator, you live in a treasure trove of memories and experiences that have accumulated over time. Every role you undertake presents opportunities that invite you to think about the educator you once were and the educator you aspire to be. If you have been entrusted with the opportunity to impact and influence the lives of kids, you are a leader. Yes, you are. Throughout your journey, you have established and developed relationships, garnered a multitude of teaching and learning practices, and taken part in conversations that have left an indelible mark on the lives of families, colleagues, and students fortunate enough to cross paths with you. You are a leader.

As you proceed with your life and continue to find the leader inside yourself and others, you will encounter new opportunities and people who eagerly await your presence. A team of people yet to be met will inevitably become a constant in your life. Others may briefly grace your path, but each serves as a signpost, guiding you toward unexplored leadership horizons. Embrace every experience, for they collectively mold the educator you aspire to become—one whose impact on the world will resonate far beyond the classroom walls. The people you meet will guide you and create pathways that lead to the discovery of opportunities you have yet to know exist. Every experience you will ever encounter leads to the type of educator you wish to become.

When you make an effort to continually build connections with people, it becomes an intrinsic act of gratitude, a deep appreciation for the journey. So, let's revisit the James Clear quote: "Your life bends in the direction of your habits. Every action you take is a vote for the person you want to become." When I reflect on my past and present experiences, I will continue to ask myself, *Who is the leader you wish*

*The Leader Inside*

to become, Lauren? My answer will continue to be, *I wish to become the leader I always needed.* I will always be grateful for the leaders who have encouraged me to lead from the past, present, and future. Remember this—no matter where your journey takes you, your actions create a collection of stories; living inside them are small intentional moves that can positively impact others. It's an impact that will move with you no matter what direction you choose to take. So, be the narrator of your story. Create what you want to be. Hold onto the memories and people who recognize your gifts. There is a leader that lives inside you. You've got this. I believe in you.

# Endnotes

1. George Couros, "4 Ways We Can Share Our Stories to Drive Innovation," November 22, 2020, in *The Innovator's Mindset* podcast, https://www.youtube.com/watch?v=hVo7mhT56xcandlist=PLQJE_z8wFZqB2h_ovgB15pbifknQOMS41andindex=38.
2. Denisa R. Superville, "7 Ways Districts Can Increase the Number of Women Leaders," *Education Week*, April 27, 2023.
3. James Clear, *Atomic Habits: An Easy and Proven Way to Build Good Habits and Break Bad Ones* (New York: 2018), 38.
4. Thomas C. Murray, *Personal and Authentic: Designing Learning Experiences That Impact a Lifetime* (San Diego: IMPress, 2019).
5. Brené Brown, "Adam Grant and Simon Sinek on What's Happening at Work, Part 1," October 3, 2022, in *Dare to Lead* podcast.
6. Stephen M. R. Covey, *Trust and Inspire: How Truly Great Leaders Unleash Greatness in Others* (New York: 2022), 35.
7. George Couros, *Because of a Teacher: Stories of the Past to Inspire the Future of Education* (San Diego: IMPress, 2021).
8. George Couros, *Because of a Teacher Volume II: Stories from the First Years of Teaching* (San Diego: IMPress, 2022), 11.
9. David Brooks, *How to Know a Person: The Art of Seeing Others Deeply and Being Deeply Seen* (New York: Random House, 2023), 9–10.
10. Covey, *Trust and Inspire*, 36.
11. Elena Aguilar, TheBrightMorningTeam.com, accessed March 28, 2024, https://assets-global.website-files.com/650894a3e9899e1797d705ee/6578f6bcfadb289687b7a6c5_Coaching%20Stems_Art%20of%20Coaching.pdf.
12. Julie Schmidt Hasson, *Safe, Seen, and Stretched: The Remarkable Ways Teachers Shape Students' Lives* (New York: Routledge, 2022), 3.
13. Sean Gaillard, "#SafeSeenStretched with Julie Hasson," January 22, 2022, in *Principal Liner Notes* podcast, https://podcasters.spotify.com/pod/show/sean-gaillard/episodes/SafeSeenStretched-with-Julie-Hasson-e1da741/a-a79dvk9.
14. Adam Grant, "Admiral Linda Fagan on Servant Leadership," May 30, 2023, in *ReThinking with Adam Grant* podcast, https://open.spotify.com/episode/2zLXJOrX8kdF0eABSXxT9q?si=zVtjq3ZyQPSvATSCUob_Kw.

15. Simon Sinek, *The Infinite Game* (United Kingdom: Penguin Random House, 2019).
16. Jim Knight, "Seven Principles for True Partnership," *ASCD,* August 29, 2022.
17. George Couros, Digital Portfolio Master Course, Teachable, https://george-couros-school.teachable.com/p/how-to-create-and-use-digital-portfolios.
18. Elisabeth Bostwick and Lauren Kaufman, "Making Podcasts Part of Professional Learning," Edutopia, October 27, 2023, https://www.edutopia.org/article/bringing-podcasts-into-professional-learning/.
19. Lauren Kaufman and Stephanie Rothstein, "Taking Control of Your Professional Growth," Edutopia, July 14, 2021, https://www.edutopia.org/article/taking-control-your-professional-growth/.
20. Brené Brown, "Brené with Simon Sinek on Developing an Infinite Mindset," January 18, 2021, in *Dare to Lead* podcast, https://brenebrown.com/podcast/brene-with-simon-sinek-on-developing-an-infinite-mindset/
21. Clear, *Atomic Habits*, 38.
22. Brené Brown, *Atlas of the Heart: Mapping Meaningful Connection and Language of Human Experience* (New York: Random House, 2021), 42–43.
23. Dr. Rachel George and Majalise W. Yolanda, *She Leads: The Women's Guide to a Career in Educational Leadership* (San Diego: Dave Burgess Consulting, 2022), 41.
24. Ryan Holiday, *The Obstacle Is the Way: The Timeless Art of Turning Trials Into Triumph* (New York: Penguin Group, 2014),10.
25. *NYS Program Guidance and Standards for Mentoring*, accessed February 3, 2024, https://www.nysed.gov/sites/default/files/nysed-mentoring-standards-and-program-guidance_0523.pdf.
26. Couros, *Innovator's Mindset*. 2.
27. Dr. Joe Sanfilippo, *Lead from Where You Are: Building Intention, Connection, and Direction in Our Schools* (San Diego: IMPress, 2022), 15.
28. Sanfilippo, 17.
29. Couros, *Because of a Teacher Volume II*, 5.
30. Couros, *Innovator's Mindset*, 52.
31. Murray, *Personal and Authentic*. 2-18.
32. Lauren Kaufman, "Unlocking Significant Moments in Time," May 11, 2020, https://laurenmkaufman.com/2020/05/11/__trashed-4/.
33. Brené Brown, "Brené with Jim Collins on Curiosity, Generosity, and the Hedgehog," December 14, 2020, in *Dare to Lead* podcast, https://

brenebrown.com/podcast/brene-with-jim-collins-on-curiosity-generosity-and-the-hedgehog/.

34. Jim Collins, *Good to Great* (New York: Harper Collins, 2001), 62.
35. Shawn Achor, *Big Potential: How Transforming the Pursuit of Success Raises Our Achievement, Happiness, and Well-Being* (New York: Crown Currency, 2018), 21.
36. Achor, 20–21.
37. Brown, "Brené with Jim Collins," https://brenebrown.com/podcast/brene-with-jim-collins-on-curiosity-generosity-and-the-hedgehog/.
38. Covey, *Trust and Inspire*, 32.
39. Jim Knight, "The Beautiful Question," ASCD, December 1, 2022, https://www.ascd.org/el/articles/the-beautiful-question.
40. Don Miguel Ruiz, *The Four Agreements: A Practical Guide to Personal Freedom* (San Rafael, CA: Amber-Allen Publishing, 1997), 26, 28, 32.
41. Miriam Plotinsky, *Lead Like a Teacher: How to Elevate Expertise in Your School* (New York: W.W. Norton and Company, 2023), 6.
42. Plotinsky, 6.
43. Holiday, *Obstacle Is the Way*, 16.
44. Couros, *Innovator's Mindset*, 79.
45. Lainie Rowell, *Evolving with Gratitude: Small Practices in Learning Communities that Make a Big Difference with Kids, Peers, and the World* (San Diego: IMPress, 2022), 96.
46. "TheStudentExperience21," Battelle for Kids, August 20, 2023, https://www.battelleforkids.org/how-we-help/the-student-experience21.
47. Brene Brown, Braving the Wilderness: The Quest for True Belonging and the Courage to Stand Alone (New York: Random House, 2017), 147.
48. Shawn Achor, "The Happy Secret to Better Work," filmed February 1, 2012. Bloomington, IN, TED video, 9:54 to 10:28, https://www.ted.com/talks/shawn_achor_the_happy_secret_to_better_work.
49. Meghan Lawson, *Legacy of Learning: Teaching for Lasting Impact* (San Diego: IMPress, 2023), 56.
50. Clear, *Atomic Habits*, 15.

# About Lauren Kaufman

**Lauren M. Kaufman** is an educator whose passion lies in empowering fellow educators to lead, share their gifts with others, and foster lifelong literacy practices in all learners. With nearly two decades of experience in education, she has held various roles, including elementary classroom teacher, elementary and middle school literacy specialist, instructional coach, mentor coordinator K–12, and assistant principal. Currently, she serves as a district leader and holds the position of director of literacy K–12 in Long Island, New York. Lauren has spearheaded numerous projects, including the development of seventy-five Units of Study in reading and writing for K–5, and has implemented a comprehensive approach to literacy. She is dedicated to providing educators with job-embedded professional learning opportunities and supporting new teachers in acclimating to the school system's culture and climate. Lauren values collaboration and is committed to sharing best instructional practices with colleagues, fostering powerful professional learning communities and networks that cultivate meaningful, relevant learning and growth.

Lauren consistently shares her passion for learning by speaking at national and local conferences, blogging on her own platform, and participating in podcasts; she also contributed to *Because of a Teacher* by George Couros and *Evolving with Gratitude* by Lainie Rowell. She has authored chapters in educational journals, and her writing has been highlighted in Edutopia, *Education Week*, Defined Learning, and Future Ready Schools.

**Connect with Lauren:**
LaurenMKaufman.com
Social Media: @LaurenMKaufman
#TheLeaderInside

# Acknowledgments

Six years ago, I had the privilege of connecting with George Couros. One of my favorite quotes from George is, "Change is the opportunity to do something amazing!" George encouraged me to start blogging to share my learning, for which I am eternally grateful. His guidance and encouragement have given me the confidence to embark on this journey. I never could have imagined that I'd write a book, let alone maintain a blog. Thank you, George, for giving me the wings to help me fly.

Paige Couros, I am very grateful for your guidance, patience, and belief in me throughout this process. Your role as a compassionate sounding board has been invaluable. Thank you for generously providing me with this empowering space to share my journey.

To my parents, Bob and Susan Epstein, who have been the cornerstone of inspiration for this book. As my first teachers, they exemplify the epitome of human kindness, serve as role models, and embody educational excellence. Their unwavering support and belief in me have shaped me into the person and leader I am now and the one I am still becoming.

To my sister, Brooke, your kindness and exceptional talent as an educator and mother are unparalleled. Your ability to connect with students at the onset of their educational path through empathy, song, and love is truly remarkable.

To my beloved grandparents, Goldie, Bill, David, and Pat, your storytelling and steadfast belief in me have deeply ingrained within me the cherished values of family, leadership, and love. My heartfelt gratitude extends especially to my late dear Grandpa David, a former educator, attorney, and author whose profound wisdom and passion for education serve as eternal beacons of inspiration. Your collective presence in my life has empowered me to discover and nurture the leader within.

To my cherished family and friends, throughout my journey, I've been blessed with a sea of educators and steadfast people who have remained constants in my world. Your presence has been an anchor, grounding me through life's ebbs and flows. You hold a special place in my heart, and your support and love have been invaluable.

To Dave Burgess, Sean Gaillard, Adam Welcome, Thomas C. Murray, and Dr. Mary Hemphill, your support and mentorship have been a guiding force from the outset. Your words of wisdom and encouragement have fueled my confidence in embracing the vital work in education.

Thank you to the IMPress editorial team, in particular Lindsey Alexander for being so responsive to my questions and making the entire revision process manageable and seamless. Your care and attention to detail was instrumental in ensuring the success of this project, and I am deeply grateful for your dedication and expertise.

To the DBC Inc. team, your dedication and commitment to your authors are truly admirable. Your unique ability to celebrate and amplify the voices of others is deeply valued and appreciated.

To my inspiring contributors, friends, and mentors, Lainie Rowell, Stephanie Rothstein, Natasha Nurse, Linda Roth (whom I mention specifically and wholeheartedly throughout this book), and Meghan Lawson, your invaluable contributions to this book have touched me deeply. I am profoundly honored that you chose to share your journeys within these pages. Your presence, dedication, and commitment to education inspire me daily. Without your beautiful words, this book would not have been possible. Thank you from the bottom of my heart.

To Beth Longo, Karen Sauter, Brenda Young, Dr. Paul Romanelli, Lorie Beard, Sean Murray, Dr. Kusum Sinha, Nan McLaughlin, Chris Hartigan, Lyn McKay, and all the leadership teams, teachers, and students I have had the privilege to work with over the years, thank you for recognizing the gifts within me I may have not recognized in myself. You are lanterns that have guided me toward paths I didn't know existed on this transformative journey.

To Natasha Nurse and Christine LaMarca, my dear friends and fellow instructional coaches, your genuine friendship has been a pillar of support in my life. Together, we have shared laughter, learning, tears, and meaningful collaborations that have enriched my journey immeasurably.

To all the educators, readers, and those I have yet to meet on this journey, your belief in yourself and dedication to inspiring others epitomize personal and professional growth. As we navigate the ever-evolving landscape of education, remember that the door of transformation is always open. Embrace the inspiration and optimism from those around you, recognizing that you are your own life vest, prepared to navigate the boundless sea of possibilities. Together, we are poised to swim, thrive, and make a meaningful difference.

And finally, to my husband, Josh, and beautiful boys, Drew and Ethan. You have taught me the meaning of loving and leading with heart in everything I do. Thank you for your patience and support as I have navigated my professional journey and for giving me space to spend many of my days writing and finding the leader within.

With gratitude and deep appreciation,
Lauren

# More books from IMPRESS

*Empower: What Happens When Students Own Their Learning* by A.J. Juliani and John Spencer

*Learner-Centered Innovation: Spark Curiosity, Ignite Passion, and Unleash Genius* by Katie Martin

*Unleash Talent: Bringing Out the Best in Yourself and the Learners You Serve* by Kara Knollmeyer

*Reclaiming Our Calling: Hold On to the Heart, Mind, and Hope of Education* by Brad Gustafson

*Take the L.E.A.P.: Ignite a Culture of Innovation* by Elisabeth Bostwick

*Drawn to Teach: An Illustrated Guide to Transforming Your Teaching* written by Josh Stumpenhorst and illustrated by Trevor Guthke

*Math Recess: Playful Learning in an Age of Disruption* by Sunil Singh and Dr. Christopher Brownell

*Innovate inside the Box: Empowering Learners Through UDL and Innovator's Mindset* by George Couros and Katie Novak

*Personal & Authentic: Designing Learning Experiences That Last a Lifetime* by Thomas C. Murray

*Learner-Centered Leadership: A Blueprint for Transformational Change in Learning Communities* by Devin Vodicka

*Kids These Days: A Game Plan for (Re)Connecting with Those We Teach, Lead, & Love* by Dr. Jody Carrington

*UDL and Blended Learning: Thriving in Flexible Learning Landscapes* by Katie Novak and Catlin Tucker

## The Leader Inside

*Teachers These Days: Stories & Strategies for Reconnection* by Dr. Jody Carrington and Laurie McIntosh

*Because of a Teacher: Stories of the Past to Inspire the Future of Education* written and curated by George Couros

*Because of a Teacher, Volume 2: Stories from the First Years of Teaching* written and curated by George Couros

*Evolving Education: Shifting to a Learner-Centered Paradigm* by Katie Martin

*Adaptable: How to Create an Adaptable Curriculum and Flexible Learning Experiences That Work in Any Environment* by A.J. Juliani

*Lead from Where You Are: Building Intention, Connection, and Direction in Our Schools* by Joe Sanfelippo

*The Shift to Student-Led: Reimagining Classroom Workflows with UDL and Blended Learning* by Catlin R. Tucker & Katie Novak

*The Design Thinking Classroom: Using Design Thinking to Reimagine the Role and Practice of Educators* by David Jakes

*Shift Writing into the Classroom with UDL and Blended Learning* by Catlin R. Tucker and Katie Novak

*Teach Happy: Small Steps to Big Joy* by Kim Strobel

*What Makes a Great Principal* by George Couros and Allyson Apsey

www.ingramcontent.com/pod-product-compliance
Lightning Source LLC
Chambersburg PA
CBHW060156190426
43199CB00044B/2640